THIS IS
AUSTRALIA

THIS IS
AUSTRALIA

Text by Bruce Elder

Published in Australia by
New Holland Publishers (Australia) Pty Ltd
Sydney • Auckland • London • Cape Town

14 Aquatic Drive Frenchs Forest NSW 2086 Australia
1A/218 Lake Road Northcote Auckland New Zealand
24 Nutford Place London W1H 6DQ United Kingdom
80 McKenzie Street Cape Town 8001 South Africa

First published in 1996
Reprinted 1997, 1999

ISBN 1 86436 204 9 (hardcover) and ISBN 1 86436 205 7 (softcover)

Publishing Manager: Mariëlle Renssen
Project Manager and Edit
Copy Editor: Robyn Flemming
Editorial Assistant: Jacquie Brown
Senior Designer: Peter Bosman
Picture Researcher: Vicki Hastrich
Illustrator: Loretta Chegwidden
DTP Cartographer: John Loubser
Reproduction by cmyk prepress
Printed and bound in Singapore by Tien Wah Press (Pte) Ltd

Frontispiece: *Australia has the world's second largest desert area. From Western Australia
to places like Windorah in western Queensland, sand dunes endlessly rise and fall.*
Title page: *Covering 215 000 square kilometres and stretching along the Queensland coast for
about 2000 kilometres, the Great Barrier Reef is one of Australia's greatest natural wonders.*
Acknowledgments page: *The kangaroo has become a symbol of Australia's unique wildlife.*
Content's page: *The expression 'sun, sand and surf' aptly describes Queensland's Gold Coast,
one of the country's most popular holiday destinations.*

PHOTOGRAPHIC ACKNOWLEDGMENTS

Shaen Adey/NHAIL acknowledgments page, p13, p17, p31 (top), p35, p55, p75, p77 (top and bottom), p84 (top left), p86, p87 (top and bottom), p88 (top), p89 (bottom), p90 (top), p91 (top), pp90-91, p92, p93 (top and middle), p94 (top and bottom), p96, p97 (top, bottom left and right), p99 (top left, and bottom), p100 (top and bottom), p171 (top), back cover (inset left) **APL** p62, p63 (bottom), p103 (bottom), p155 (top left), p161 **John Baker/APL** p68 (bottom), p119, p136 **J.P. & E.S. Baker/APL** p112 **John W. Banagan/The Image Bank** p71 (top) **Ross Barnett/APL** p66 **Ira Block/The Image Bank** p26 **Ian Brown** p101 **Ian Brown/HJPL** p102 (bottom) **John Carnemolla/APL** p19, p29, p38, p68 (top), pp116-117, p172 **Amanda Clement/The Image Bank** p18 (left) **Evan Collis/APL** pp168-169 **J.M. Cornish** p150 (top) **Michael Coyne/The Image Bank** front cover (inset right) **Tom & Pam Gardner** p149 (bottom) **P. German** p15 (bottom), p18 (right), p20 (top), p23, p24 (top), p126 (top left), p141 (bottom), p171 (bottom) **Denise Greig/NHAIL** back cover (inset centre) **Tony Gwynn-Jones** p74 (bottom), p85 (bottom), p89 (top), p102 (top) **Peter Henry/The Image Bank** p137 (top) **Wally Herzfeld/APL** p142-143 **Owen Hughes/APL** p160, p166 (top) **Anthony Johnson/NHAIL** front cover (main photograph, inset centre), title page, contents page, p15 (top), p31 (bottom), p36, p40, p43, p48, p51, p53, p56, p57, p60 (bottom), p61 (bottom), p65, p78, p79, p80 (top), p81 (top, bottom left and right), p82, p84 (bottom right), p85 (top), p93 (bottom), p95, p98, p104, p105, p106 (left and right), p107 (top and bottom), p108 (top left and right, and bottom), p109, p110 (bottom), p122 (bottom left and right), p123 (top and bottom), p128, p130, p131 (top and bottom), p133, p134, p135 (top and bottom left and right), p144, p145, p146 (bottom left and right), p147 (top and bottom), p148 (top), p152 bottom), p153 (top and bottom), p154, p155 (bottom), p156 (right), p158, p159, p162 (top and bottom), p163 (top and bottom), p164 (bottom), p165 **Tony Joyce/APL** p42 **Tom Keating/Wildlight** p14, p174 **Noeline Kelly/APL** p115 **Ford Kristo** p22 **Ian Lever** p64 (top), p69, p74 (top), p103 (top), p152 (top), p156 (left), p157, p164 (top), p166 (bottom), p167 (top) **Gary Lewis/APL** p10 **Lightstorm/APL** pp72-73, p140 (bottom), p141 (top), **Jonathan Marks/APL** frontispiece, p138 (bottom), **Aureo Martelli/APL** p12, p67 **Leo Meier/APL** p27, p76, p170, **National Library of Australia** p25, p33 **Robbi Newman/The Image Bank** p167 (bottom) **F. Prenzel/APL** p114 (bottom right) **Philip Quirk/Wildlight** p21 **Nick Rains** p54, p60 (top), p61 (left), p64 (bottom left and bottom), p127, p139, back cover (inset right) **Nick Rains/APL** front cover (inset left), p132 **Mark Rajkovic** p121 **Chris Raphael/APL** p37 **L.F. Schick/Australian Museum** p24 (bottom) **Brian Scott/APL** p20 (bottom) **Joe Shemesh** pp58-59, p63 (left), p70 (top), p71 (bottom), p80 (right), p113 (bottom), p120, p124, p125 (top right and bottom), p126 (top right and bottom), p129 **NHAIL** p16, p34, p39, p41, p45, p46, p70 (bottom), p110 (top), p114 (top), p122 (top left), p148 (bottom), p149 (top), spine **Paul Sinclair** p8 (top), p83, p111, p114 (bottom left), p118 (top and bottom), p154 **SLNSW** p30, p32, p47, p49, p50 **Paul Steel** p8 (bottom), p140 (top), p150 (bottom), p151, p155 (top right), p173 **Oliver Strewe/APL** p52, p84 (bottom left) **Jann Subiaco/APL** p44 **Cherie Vasas** p99 (top right) **Steve Vidler/APL** p88 (bottom), p113 (top) **Dave Watts/Australian Museum** p125 (top left) **Neale Winter/APL** p138 (top) **David Witts/Wildlight** p137 (bottom)

The following abbreviations have been used:
SLNSW State Library of New South Wales
APL Australian Picture Library
HJPL High Jinx Photo Library
NHAIL New Holland Australia Image Library

CONTENTS

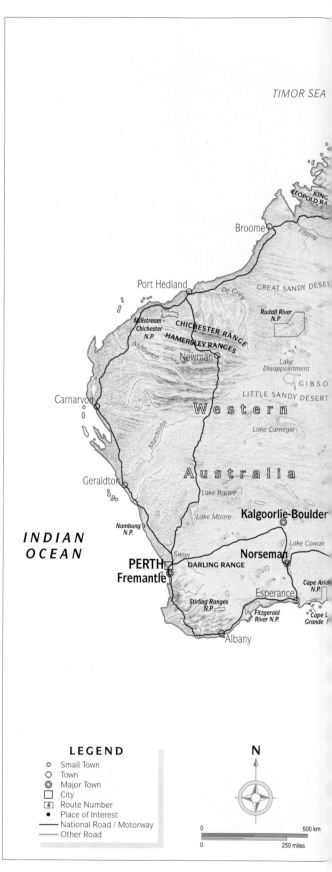

Top: The Great Ocean Road in Victoria is one of Australia's most beautiful coastal stretches. Particularly impressive are the formations known as the Twelve Apostles, sandstone remnants of a coastline weathered by the mighty Southern Ocean.
Bottom: Hundreds of strange rock formations, the Pinnacles were created by a combination of wind, rain and the cementing agent, calcium. The rocks pierce through the sand dunes near Cervantes in Western Australia.

TIMOR SEA

INDIAN OCEAN

Broome

Port Hedland

De Grey

GREAT SANDY DESEI

Rudall River N.P.

Millstream - Chichester N.P.

CHICHESTER RANGE

Ashburton

HAMERSLEY RANGES

Newman

Lake Disappointment

GIBSO

Carnarvon

LITTLE SANDY DESERT

Murchison

W e s t e r n

Lake Carnegie

A u s t r a l i a

Geraldton

Lake Barlee

Lake Moore

Kalgoorlie-Boulder

Nambung N.P.

Lake Cowan

Norseman

Swan

DARLING RANGE

Cape Arid N.P.

PERTH
Fremantle

Esperance

Stirling Ranges N.P.

Fitzgerald River N.P.

Cape L Grande N

Albany

KING
LEOPOLD RA.

Fitzroy

LEGEND

- ○ Small Town
- ○ Town
- ◎ Major Town
- ☐ City
- [4] Route Number
- • Place of Interest
- —— National Road / Motorway
- —— Other Road

N

0   500 km

0   250 miles

ARAFURA SEA

DARWIN

Litchfield N.P.
Kakadu N.P.
Drysdale River N.P.
Lake Argyle
DURACK RANGE
Purnululu N.P.
BUNGLE BUNGLE RANGE

ARNHEM LAND

Nitmiluk (Katherine Gorge) N.P.
Roper
Victoria

Gregory National Park

TANAMI DESERT

BARKLY TABLELAND

Northern

Territory

Tennant Creek

DAVENPORT RANGE

Lake Mackay

West Mac-Donnell N.P.
Alice Springs
Finke Gorge N.P.
MACDONNELL RANGES
Lake Neale
Lake Amadeus
Uluru Kata Tjuta N.P.

DESERT
PETERMANN RANGES

SIMPSON DESERT

GREAT VICTORIA DESERT

Witjira N.P.

South

STURTS STONY DESERT

Coober Pedy

Australia

NULLARBOR PLAIN
Nullarbor Regional Reserve
Yellabinna Regional Reserve
Nullarbor N.P.
Ceduna
Lake Gairdner

Woomera
Lake Torrens

Lake Eyre N.P.
Lake Eyre
Cooper
Lake Frome

Gammon Ranges N.P.
FLINDERS RANGES
Flinders Ranges N.P.

Port Augusta

Great Australian Bight

Port Lincoln
ADELAIDE

Mount Gambier

GULF of Carpentaria

CAPE YORK PENINSULA

Jardine River N.P.

Great Barrier Reef

SOUTH PACIFIC OCEAN

Lakefield N.P.

ATHERTON TABLELAND

Mitchell

Daintree N.P.
Cairns

CORAL SEA

Lawn Hill N.P.
Flinders

Mount Isa

Queensland

Longreach

Diamantina N.P.

Simpson Desert N.P.
Diamantina

Townsville

Great Barrier Reef

Mackay

GREAT DIVIDING RANGE
Burdekin

Rockhampton

Bundaberg
Great Sandy N.P.

Carnarvon Gorge N.P.

Sturt N.P.

Mootwingee N.P.

New South

Warrumbungle N.P.

BRISBANE

Oxley Wild Rivers N.P.

Wollemi N.P.

Wales
GREAT DIVIDING RANGE

Lake Mungo N.P.

Newcastle

Blue Mtns N.P.
SYDNEY
Kanangra Boyd N.P.
Wollongong
CANBERRA
A.C.T.

Murray-Sunset Country

Wyperfeld N.P.

Victoria

Grampians N.P.

Alpine N.P.
Mt Kosciusko N.P.

Snowy River N.P.

TASMAN SEA

Otway N.P.
MELBOURNE
Wilsons Promontory N.P.

Tasmania

Cradle Mtn-Lake St Clair N.P.
Launceston
Franklin-Gordon Wild Rivers N.P.
Freycinet N.P.
Southwest N.P.
HOBART

SOUTHERN OCEAN

9

PROFILE OF AUSTRALIA

Australia is both the world's largest island and its smallest continent. Covering an area of 7 682 300 square kilometres, it lies between the latitudes of 10°41'S (Cape York in Queensland) and 43°39'S (South Cape in Tasmania). The distance between these northern and southern extremities is 3680 kilometres. The continent stretches over a greater latitudinal range than the United States and is slightly smaller than the north—south range of Europe from Finland to Greece.

Longitudinally the country is larger than Europe and slightly smaller than the United States, stretching from Steep Point on the Western Australian coast (113°09'E) to Cape Byron in New South Wales (153°39'E), a distance of approximately 4000 kilometres.

Given its size, it is not surprising that Australia is a land of great climatic and topographic diversity. It ranges from the dense tropical rainforests and mangrove swamps of northern Queensland through the broad savanna grasslands of eastern Australia, the alpine zones of the Snowy Mountains which straddle southern New South Wales and northern Victoria, to the vast deserts of central Australia which extend westward to the central coastline of Western Australia.

The first Aborigines arrived from the Indonesian archipelago some 55 000 years ago; over the next 15 000 years, they spread throughout the continent. It was not until the end of the 18th century that the British explored, and subsequently settled, the continent's fertile eastern coast. Although the French explored the coastline a few years later, they did not establish any settlements; consequently, modern-day Australia is the only continent which is also a single, unified country.

Modern-day Australia consists of six states, two major territories and eight small, external territories. The largest state is Western Australia which, with an area of 2 525 500 square kilometres, accounts for approximately one-third of the continent's landmass.

Nearly 60 per cent of Australia's population lives in New South Wales (which covers 810 600 square kilometres, or 10 per cent of the continent) and Victoria (227 600 square kilometres or 2.96 per cent).

Australia administers seven external territories. Lying to the north of New Zealand and east of the coast of New South Wales is Norfolk Island. Discovered by Captain James Cook in 1774, the island initially served as a penal colony from 1788 to 1814 and again from 1825 to 1855. In 1856 the descendants of the *Bounty* mutineers were transferred to the island from their home on Pitcairn Island. It was subsequently placed under the jurisdiction of the Governor of New South Wales and in 1913 became a territory of the Commonwealth of Australia.

Opposite: There are only a few remnants of the great rainforests that once covered most of northern and eastern Australia.

Lying 4100 kilometres south-west of Perth on the icy edges of Antarctica is the territory of Heard and McDonald Islands. These rocky outcrops became an Australian territory in 1947 and since then, although uninhabited, have been used periodically for scientific research.

Australia's Antarctic Territory covers 5.8 million square kilometres—an area roughly equivalent to Western Australia, Queensland, the Northern Territory and Victoria combined. This is the area south of latitude 60°S, between longitudes 45°E and 160°E, and excluding a sliver of French territory known as Terre Adélie which lies between longitudes 136°E and 142°E. The territory is used primarily for scientific research and now has a number of permanent settlements. Mawson and Davis are the most important of these settlements, with a population which falls to around 70 in the winter and rises to approximately 200 in the summer months.

Located 2768 kilometres north-west of Perth and roughly due west of Broome, the Cocos (Keeling) Islands are a group of 27 coral islands which were settled by John Clunies-Ross in 1827. Australia assumed responsibility for the administration of the islands in 1955.

To the east of the Cocos Islands lies Christmas Island—a small island of 135 square kilometres with a population of around 1000 people of Chinese and Malay descent—and the uninhabited Ashmore and Cartier Islands.

In 1969 all the uninhabited islands east of the Great Barrier Reef to longitude 156°06'E and bounded by latitudes 12°S and 24°S became an Australian territory.

In recent times, Australia's two internal territories—the Northern Territory and the Australian Capital Territory—have become self-governing. This leaves the tiny territory at Jervis Bay, situated on the New South Wales south coast, as the only remaining internal territory administered by the Commonwealth Government. Originally created as a port facility, today Jervis Bay comprises an Aboriginal community at Wreck Bay, a naval facility (HMAS *Creswell*), a few small private leases, and a national park which occupies 80 per cent of the land.

THE LAND

Australia is the oldest and most stable of all the continents. Originally part of a vast southern landmass known as Gondwana, there are areas of the country where geologists have estimated that the rocks are 4500 million years old.

Around 100 million years ago, the Gondwana landmass separated from Antarctica and moved northward. Twenty million years later the island groups of Australasia, most notably New Zealand and New Caledonia, split from the larger continent.

For 80 million years rain, sun, ice and wind have eroded the mountain ranges so that Australia is now the flattest and lowest continent on earth. At the same time, there were no significant tectonic forces operating on the continent that would have caused new mountains to be formed. The result is some remarkable landforms. Mount Kosciusko, the highest mountain peak in the whole of Australia, is only 2228 metres above sea level.

The rocky outcrops of central Australia are vast mountain ranges reduced to small hills by aeons of weathering. Uluru (Ayers Rock), for example, is a remnant of an eroded mountain range. Similarly, the MacDonnell Ranges which sprawl to the east and west of Alice Springs are so weathered they are like the exposed bare bones of the earth.

Continental Australia can be divided into three clearly defined geological areas. The Western Plateau (sometimes referred to as the Western Craton) stretches from outback Queensland to the coast of Western Australia and includes the vast Great Sandy, Gibson and Great Victoria deserts as well as the ancient plateaux in the Kimberley, Arnhem and Hamersley regions. This is the oldest part of the continent and it has existed as a landmass for over 500 million years.

Above: *The climb to the top of Australia's highest mountain, Mount Kosciusko, is a pleasant 6-kilometre walk from a nearby chairlift. Bushwalking is ideal here in summer, and in winter the snowfields are very popular for skiing and snowboarding.*

To the east, running from the Gulf of Carpentaria south to Victoria and South Australia, are the Central Lowlands which include the Murray–Darling Plains and the Great Artesian Basin. This is flat, inhospitable, marginal land characterised by eroded mountain ranges, vast salt lakes, sand dunes and extensive sedimentary deposits.

Rising gently from the Central Lowlands, the Eastern Highlands are a series of plateaux and low mountain ranges running the length of the eastern coast of the continent. The most prominent feature is the Great Dividing Range which is notable for its small waterfalls and the rivers which flow west from the range towards the Central Lowlands.

The Eastern Highlands drop away rapidly to a coastal plain which, in turn, gives way to rocky headlands, beautiful sandy beaches, extensive coastal wetlands and rich, fertile coastal plains watered by the short rivers which rise in the highlands. This is where most of Australia's population lives. It is also the agricultural heartland of the country, with the lowlands being ideal dairy and beef cattle country and the coastal plains suitable for crops that include sugarcane, pineapples and bananas.

THE CLIMATE

The Australian continent is characterised by great climatic variation. Its size and latitudinal range produce climates which range from steamy tropics to cold, dry continentality (continentality occurs in regions that are situated beyond the moderating influence of the sea and it results in low levels of precipitation and temperature extremes).

The tropics which stretch across the north of the continent give way to subtropical and temperate conditions along the eastern coast. The Snowy Mountains in southern New South Wales and the highlands of Tasmania experience alpine conditions while the vast 'dead heart', which extends from the Western Australian coast across to south-west Queensland and north-west New South Wales, is arid desert. Australia is a very dry continent. It is second only to Antarctica, where the annual precipita-

Above: *People escape the cool southern winters by flocking to the Great Barrier Reef where, every day, cruises to the Outer Reef offer snorkelling and scuba diving for travellers eager to see the world-renowned tropical fish and coral gardens.*

tion level is less than 50 millimetres. More than half of Australia receives less than 300 millimetres of rainfall a year. This extreme dryness is exacerbated by the dramatic effects of continentality. In Alice Springs, for example, it is common for temperatures to soar above 35°C during the day and drop below freezing at night.

Most of Australia experiences tropical and subtropical conditions. The most distinctive climates include 'the wet' which sweeps across the north of the country in early summer; the dry extreme continentality which affects the centre; the mild Mediterranean climate of wet winters and long dry summers which makes areas of South Australia and Western Australia so perfect for vineyards; and, lastly, the balmy tropical winters and cyclonic summers which characterise the northern coasts of Queensland and Western Australia.

'The wet' is the result of warm, moist monsoonal air moving south from the equator and passing across northern Australia. The season is clearly defined. In September and October the humidity begins to rise until the climate in centres like Darwin and Katherine is oppressive and unpleasant. Finally 'the wet' arrives; it is characterised by awe-inspiring atmospheric displays of thunder and

lightning and drenching monsoonal rains. These rains fill the rivers and wetlands of the north and, because they come in early summer, result in rapid vegetation growth.

In spite of the regular rains in the north, most of Australia is vulnerable to extended drought conditions. The desert region starts on the Western Australian coast and extends east to the western parts of Queensland and New South Wales. So dry is the desert area that it is recognised as the world's second-largest hot desert area after the Sahara. The problem is that moist air masses rarely reach the continental centre; consequently there is an average of two days of rain a month.

The dryness of the continent is also exacerbated by the El Niño, a condition which occurs when there are abnormally warm surface waters in the tropical Pacific. It produces an extended period of dryness over the northern part of the continent. This has flow-on effects, because the rains which would normally flow into the vast Murray–Darling river system do not arrive and consequently large areas of western New South Wales and Queensland are adversely affected.

Most of the densely populated areas of southern Australia experience a modified Mediterranean climate, which

Above: *William Dampier, the first Englishman to sight the Pilbara region of Western Australia, described it as 'barren towards the Sea, and affording me neither fresh Water, nor any great Store of other Refreshments'. This dry coastal desert only changes when the cyclonic storm clouds from the north bring temporary relief.*

is produced by movements in the anticyclones, or high-pressure systems, crossing the southern part of the continent. In winter the anticyclones move further north and are accompanied by cool, moist westerly winds bringing rain. In summer they move further south and bring fine, warmer weather to the region. These conditions are ideal for growing wheat and are nearly perfect for the development of vineyards. Consequently, areas of South Australia and Western Australia are known for their quality wines and the richness of their wheat production.

Most of Australia's population lives on the continent's eastern coast. While the southern coastline experiences wet winters and dry summers, further north the coast is under the influence of tropical cyclones. It is common for these cyclones to develop off the coast of Queensland between November and April each year. On average, three cyclones will directly affect the northern Queensland coast each summer. Often they will cross the coast, and can cause considerable damage and destruction if they are near population centres.

It is common, particularly around Sydney, for periods of intense summer humidity to last for a number of days before relief arrives in the form of the southerly buster—the local term for the cool stream of air which results in temperatures tumbling by up to 20 degrees in a matter of hours.

Apart from these two extremes, the summer climate over most of eastern Australia tends to be warm and sunny.

THE LAND

In the beginning

Australia has a rich diversity of unique flora and fauna. The continent has been separated from other landmasses for over 40 million years and during that time, plants and animals have evolved in isolation. They have also survived in a diverse and non-competitive environment, the result being that Australia has over 25 000 species of plants. By comparison, all of Europe (an area larger than Australia) has only 70 per cent of this number of plants.

Botanists argue that this diversity is the result of the stability of the Australian continent's climate. As the earth's temperatures changed, Australia drifted towards climatic zones which helped to keep temperatures relatively constant. This meant that species were able to survive and evolve without being confronted by the dramatic changes in climate brought on by Ice Ages and by periods of global warming.

The stability of the continent is truly remarkable. There is evidence that the iron ore deposits in the Hamersley Range of Western Australia are over 2500 million years old. Some of the rivers on the east coast have remained relatively unchanged for tens of millions of years. The flatness of the continent was not conducive to the development of glaciers during the Ice Ages, and the processes which help to produce rich soils—volcanoes, glaciers and frequent flooding—have not occurred. This means that Australia's soils are poor, leached and lacking in vital nutrients.

In order to survive in an environment affected by infertile soils and the drought ravages of the El Niño effect, Australia's plants have been forced to develop strategies where they use very few of their resources and take full advantage of the rare substantial rainfall periods. The most obvious example of these plant survival mechanisms is the predominance, particularly in areas of desert, heathland and mallee, of plants that are characterised by small, sharp leaves—notably banksias, bottlebrushes and ti-trees.

There are around 500 species of eucalypt—including both shrubs and trees—most of which are native to Australia, and it has been estimated that there are more than 600 varieties of acacia on the continent that are endemic to Australia. The *Triodia* and *Plectrachne* genera of hummock grass are widespread from western Queensland to the desert areas of the Northern Territory and Western Australia.

The nature of Australia's environment, and particularly the nature of Australian vegetation, was profoundly affected by the arrival of the Aborigines some 40 000—55 000 years ago. Certainly, by the time the Europeans arrived the Aborigines were using fire extensively. Abel Tasman, the Dutch navigator who discovered Tasmania, saw burning which lasted for days. Captain James Cook, after sailing up the east coast, referred to Australia as 'this continent of smoke' and Joseph Banks, the botanist who accompanied Cook, made frequent mention in his journals of seeing fires. While exploring central Australia, Ernest Giles wrote: 'The natives were about, burning, burning, ever burning'.

The impact of this apparent obsession with burning off the undergrowth was profound. If the descriptions of the eastern coastline provided by the journals of the First Fleeters are to be believed, burning off reduced the height of the trees and left large areas of open space. Joseph Banks's descriptions of both the area near Bulli Pass, south of Sydney, and the headlands around Botany Bay suggest the land was cleared. Today, both areas are quite densely forested.

The Aborigines used fire to set the bush alight for hunting, for signalling to other groups, to clear the ground, to hold back the southern advance of the rainforest, to kill vermin, and, most importantly, to regenerate the plants which sustained both kangaroos and humans. There is evidence that this was not a haphazard process but rather a kind of farming. In fact, the term 'firestick farming' was coined in the late 1960s to describe the phenomenon.

Perhaps the most exciting aspect of this 'firestick farming' is the notion that with the arrival of the Aborigines the

*Above: It has been estimated that Australia is home to around 500 species of gum tree, or eucalypt, which cover every corner of the country. Particularly beautiful are these river red gums (*Eucalyptus camaldulensis*), growing in the hills near Alice Springs.*

vegetation of the entire continent was changed dramatically. Fire-sensitive trees such as she-oaks and pines were replaced by fire-resistant eucalypts

By 1788, Australian vegetation consisted of closed forests, open forests, woodlands, open woodlands, scrubs and heaths, shrublands, open shrublands and herblands. As far as can be determined, the only closed forests at that time existed on the west coast of Tasmania, in a pocket south of Brisbane and in an extensive strip running north from Cairns. Open forests stretched down most of the east coast of the continent, lapped the edges of Cape York and the Northern Territory, and accounted for substantial pockets on both the east coast of Tasmania and the south-western corner of Western Australia. Woodlands ran in a vast arc from the Northern Territory through northern Queensland and down the east coast across to the west of the Great Dividing Range. There was also a substantial pocket in what is now the Western Australian wheatbelt.

The Queensland Gulf Country was characterised by open woodlands and herblands. Substantial areas of open woodlands also existed in the southern Kimberley and to the north of the Nullarbor Plain. Shrublands stretched across the Nullarbor, existed in western Victoria and accounted for a huge area

of central Western Australia; and open shrublands existed in what are now the desert areas of central Australia.

The final process of change occurred when Europeans settled the land. The impact of timber cutters, graziers clearing the land for the development of exotic, non-native pastures, as well as the extensive planting of deciduous European trees to recapture the 'beauty' of the homeland and the impact of hoofed animals all conspired to change the vegetation of temperate Australia. Today, around 60 per cent of the continent is used for livestock grazing.

Biodiversity of the rainforests

If the 'firestick farming' theory is correct, then it is likely that 100 000 years ago most of eastern and northern Australia was covered by rainforest. Palms of the species *Livistona mariae* (a variety of cabbage tree palm) are found in the Palm Valley area of the Finke Gorge National Park south of Hermannsburg in central Australia. The nearest similar palms are found on the coast of Western Australia or on the coastal strip of New South Wales. The park is home to over 400 plant types, of which more than 30 are considered rare. This is a remnant of ancient rainforest, and it may have been systematic burning off which slowly brought about the retreat of the rainforest from the centre of the continent.

Above: This acorn banksia flower occurs in Western Australia and Papua New Guinea.

These days, rainforest exists in clearly defined coastal areas with occasional pockets still occurring inland.

There are five major rainforest types. Monsoon rainforest exists in northern Western Australia and the Northern Territory and reaches across into northern Queensland. Tropical rainforest is found in a thin strip from Cape York to the Whitsunday Islands. There is also a pocket of subtropical rainforest between Brisbane and Rockhampton. A mixture of subtropical and temperate rainforest extends from Brisbane south to Kiama on the New South Wales south coast, and temperate rainforest occurs in south-eastern Victoria and along the west coast of Tasmania, particularly in the hinterland running south from Stanley to the southern tip of the island.

It is obvious that the Aborigines' fires impacted on the continent's rainforest. It is equally apparent that the rainforest varied hugely from Cape York to Tasmania, and Aboriginal dependency varied accordingly. In Tasmania, for example, the Aborigines burnt large tracts of temperate rainforest to provide fresh plants for the animal life and to clear the land so that it would become more productive. By contrast, the people who lived in the rainforests of north Queensland (predominantly the Tjapukai people) built thatched huts for protection during the rainy season, and had an intimate understanding of the hundreds of edible plants in the rainforest; it is known that they weaved the bark of the huge fig trees into blankets.

These people used the resources of the rainforest for their social and political life. Women made string-like bags for carrying produce, and men used cane to weave baskets. The bark of certain trees was used as shields, while wooden swords, and occasionally spears, were carved from the forest timbers.

Further south, in regions where the subtropical and temperate rainforest mixed, the local Aborigines tended to live in clearings and to use the rainforest as a food repository. They dug up yams and fern roots, collected the tender fresh shoots from the tree ferns, climbed the cabbage tree palms to collect the 'hearts' and ate wild fruits, particularly native limes and quandongs. While they hunted the local small animals, their primary source of food was the sea with its rich supplies of fish and crustaceans. Fishing nets were often created from the bark of the rainforest trees.

Whenever there was excess food, groups of Aborigines would gather to share the riches. These were times for celebratory corroborees and extensive social interaction. In south-east Queensland, Aborigines gathered each year to collect the nuts and cones from the bunya pines (*Araucaria bidwillii*).

Although the early settlers often referred to the rainforest as inaccessible wilderness, they were quick to destroy vast tracts by a combination of timber cutting, land clearing, mining, intensive agriculture, and the damage caused by cloven-hoofed cattle and sheep.

This rapid change in the nature of the rainforest had a devastating impact on the Aborigines who, as the delicate food chain was disturbed, found themselves facing starvation. Although they often showed the early explorers, graziers and miners ways through the rainforest, this generosity was not matched by the Europeans, who were more interested in exploiting the area.

Above: *These cabbage tree palms, found in the Palm Valley in Finke Gorge, Northern Territory, are relics from a time when central Australia was much wetter.*

The response of early travellers was more romantic than that of the graziers and timber cutters. In 1886 when the journalist Howard Willoughby wrote *Australian Pictures Drawn with Pen and Pencil*, he described the rainforest in the following glowing terms:

Beginning with the gullies of the Dandenong ranges, near Melbourne, the traveller can proceed from fairy scene to fairy scene along the coast to faraway Carpentaria and Papua, the vegetation preserving its identity, and yet slowly changing from a subtropical to a tropical character. In the Victorian region there are rivulets of clear water hidden from sight by the tree-ferns which flourish on their banks. Journeying northwards, the vegetation thickens. Parasitical ferns—the stag horns of the conservatory—grow from every branch. Palm-trees make their appearance, the noble *Livistonia* attaining in suitable places a height of eighty feet. The musktree and the *Pittosporum* scent the air, and lovely twining plants help to form impenetrable foliage.

The biodiversity of the rainforests varies significantly from north to south. The southern temperate rainforests are relatively lacking in diversity, while the tropical rainforests are rich hothouse environments of orchids, coniferous softwoods, vines and lianas, and terrestrial and epiphytic ferns.

The richest areas of rainforest occur in areas where the annual rainfall exceeds 1250 millimetres, where the soils are heavier and where the environment is relatively protected—for example, by gullies and river valleys.

The diversity of rainforest flora in Australia falls into a number of broad categories. While eucalypts do not necessarily dominate, they are an integral part of most rainforests. The forests have little ground cover. The canopy allows minimal light to penetrate to the forest floor, thus limiting photosynthesis; the heavy rainfall can often leach the nutrients that are vital for ground

Above: One of Australia's most famous areas of unspoilt rainforest is the Mossman River Gorge in the Daintree rainforest of north Queensland. This is a habitat for some of the rarest flora and fauna in the world.

foliage. Wherever a break in the forest canopy does occur, the ubiquitous lantana (an import from South America) will usually successfully fight off claims by wild ginger, inkweed, cunjevoi, raspberries, nettles and blackberries. However, there is a profusion of epiphytic vegetation—particularly ferns and orchids. Amongst the most notable of these are the king orchid, or 'rock lily', varieties of climbing ferns, bird's-nest ferns, elkhorns and staghorns.

The trees of the rainforest range from numerous varieties of fig through softwood pines to the much sought-after (although now largely cleared) quality commercial timbers such as red cedar, Queensland maple, black bean, rosewood, Antarctic beech and white beech. It is common to find lawyer vines, lianas, climbing palms and strangling figs, which are capable of growing to a height of 15 metres, attached to these trees.

Mangroves and coastal wetlands

In recent times, particularly along Australia's eastern coastline, the need to preserve the coastal wetlands has become a major environmental issue. The conflict between the desire of modern Australians to live close to the ocean and the needs of the rich wetlands along the coast has been an issue which has been fought wherever major urban development has been planned near estuaries and lakes.

Historically, river estuaries have been natural places for human settlement. Considering the size of Australia, the continent has relatively few rivers and consequently few estuarine areas. Under such circumstances it is hardly surprising that the Aborigines gravitated towards the river and lake estuaries around the coast, knowing that they would find a ready supply of crustaceans and fish, a variety of water birds as well as reliable supplies of fresh water.

The first Europeans to explore the coastline tended to stop at estuaries because they offered protected anchorage combined with easy access to food. When Captain James Cook accidentally struck the Great Barrier Reef off the coast north of Cape Tribulation, he struggled a few kilometres further north and eventually beached the HM Bark *Endeavour* on the shores of the Endeavour River; Cook and his crew were to stay on the river's foreshores from 17 June to 4 August 1770.

The first permanent European arrivals were to settle at Botany Bay but, due to difficulties in obtaining fresh water from the marshy estuary of the Cook's River, moved north to the mouth of the Tank Stream where the modern-day business metropolis of Sydney is located.

Statistics graphically demonstrate the importance of river estuaries in maintaining a delicate ecological balance. Along the New South Wales coast alone,

three-quarters of the commercial fish species are caught in estuaries; half the state's total fish catch spends at least part of its life in estuarine waters; and about 70 per cent of all crustaceans and fish caught in the state are dependent on the complex ecology of river mouths.

The vital factor in this delicate balance is the seagrass meadows which often cover the beds of estuaries. These meadows support and sustain the complex web of marine life. Young fish hide from potential predators in the dense grasses. Crustaceans live off pieces of dead seagrass. Tiny organisms eat minute particles—all of these organisms excrete and die which, in turn, fertilises the seagrass meadows. Seagrass beds are so fertile that they produce four times as much organic matter as savanna grasslands and almost as much as tropical rainforests. Damage to seagrass meadows is a constant problem as more Australians build houses and establish towns and suburbs near the coast. The damage caused by such man-made coastal developments as sewerage outlets, port and harbour facilities, sand mining and holiday recreational environments must have a major impact on commercial fishing.

Equally problematic, and equally important, are the vast mangrove swamps. In populated areas they are commonly seen as being useless and annoying. At low tide they are invariably smelly. They are the habitat of unpleasant creatures ranging from mosquitoes to crocodiles. In urban areas their dense root systems and growth patterns mean that they often trap rubbish and are used as disposal areas by irresponsible people. Mangroves also make boating and fishing difficult, as they form a swampy barrier between the shore and the open water.

Yet, in spite of all this, mangroves are dynamic ecological areas and vital feeding grounds for birds, fish and riverbank animal life. There are over 30 different varieties of mangrove growing around the coasts of Australia. The main varieties vary according to their location between the high- and low-water line. There are also major variations from the tropics to the temperate zones; thus only the grey mangrove (*Avicennia marina*) grows across the south of the continent in Victoria, South Australia and southern Western Australia, while the red mangrove (*Rhyxophora stylosa*) is common in tropical waters.

An extensive mangrove area along any of the river estuaries of Western Australia, the Northern Territory or north Queensland could typically have low, scrubby eucalypts and melaleucas growing above the high-water line. Just below the high-water mark there may be stands of spurred mangrove (*Ceriops tagal*). Beyond them will be red mangroves, and closest to the shoreline, often almost totally submerged at high tide, will be the grey mangrove. It is not uncommon for mangrove swamps in north Queensland to have up to 20 different species growing together.

The only consistent features of mangroves are their ability to survive in saturated soils and their resistance to high concentrations of salt. This resistance results in the plant either absorbing or excreting salt by storing it in its leaves, which then drop off, or by resisting salt intake through chemical actions in its roots.

Another common characteristic is the mangrove's elaborate root system, which is a result of its need for stability in soft, muddy environments. Some species have complex root systems below the estuarine mud, but it is com-

Above: *Mangroves provide a vital link in the complex ecology of many fragile coastal environments.*

Above: *Semaphore crabs live in mudflats on the edge of coastal mangrove swamps where they scavenge for food.*

mon for many species to have roots which are exposed at low tide. The red mangroves have developed roots which prop up the central trunk. Inevitably, an extensive mangrove swamp is characterised by a bewildering, anarchic forest of exposed root systems. This results in an area which is almost impenetrable to humans but ideal for catching and trapping silt (thus doing much to stabilise and extend the shoreline) and, because of its diversity, is an ideal home for a large variety of fauna. It is common in an Australian tropical mangrove swamp to find, among others, mice, crocodiles, goannas, snakes, flying foxes, mud crabs, prawns, molluscs, worms, oysters, limpets and periwinkles. With such an extensive array of fauna present, it is not all that surprising that mangroves attract vast numbers of waterfowl.

The rich flora of the desert

The image of the Sahara Desert, with its vast oceans of sand and isolated oases, is so pervasive that it is hard to imagine a desert which is anything other than endless, undulating sand dunes. Although Australia has the second-largest desert area on earth (after the Sahara), a large proportion of its desert regions is characterised by low-lying scrubby vegetation. The occasional rainstorms which blow in from the south-west can turn these desert areas into wonderlands of spectacular flowering

plants in a myriad colours and rapidly growing hardy grasses. More than 70 per cent of Australia is either arid or semi-arid. Tasmania is the only state with no desert areas at all.

The deserts vary hugely. West of Alice Springs, and stretching almost to the Western Australian coast, is the Great Sandy Desert. Viewed from the air the landscape looks like a piece of corrugated iron, with the sand dunes stretching to the horizon. Similar terrain, including 15-metre-high dunes spaced at 300- to 500-metre intervals, is characteristic of much of the Simpson Desert (south-east of Alice Springs) and the Great Victoria Desert (south-west of Alice Springs).

Closer examination reveals mound-like hummock grass growing up to a metre high and covering up to 30 per cent of the region. The most typical type of hummock grass is spinifex or 'porcupine' grass (which is any species of the genus *Triodia*), a spiny-leaved grass which helps to bind the sand together and reduce wind erosion. There are also low, scrubby shrubs of the genera *Hakea*, *Grevillea*, *Crotalaria* and *Eremophila*. This is the harshest of all the Australian deserts. It has been estimated that sandy deserts cover nearly 2 million square kilometres of the continent.

Most of the continent's sandy desert areas receive less than 250 millimetres of rainfall a year. However, these areas are known for having short-duration desert storms which activate dormant seeds and result in some of Australia's most exotic and beautiful floral displays. The desert's flowers are adapted to the harshness of the conditions. They produce large numbers of seeds which are scattered by the winds. Many of the seeds are protected by hard or chemical coatings and are so environmentally sensitive that they will resist showers and only be opened by rains heavy enough to ensure their successful germination.

There is a great diversity of desert wildflowers—everything from everlasting daisies to desert peas, vetches and pink capers. The Sturt's desert pea (*Clianthus formosus*), the floral emblem of South Australia, is notable for its shiny black central boss and rich red flowers.

Nearly 1 million square kilometres of Australia are covered by 'stony' desert. These deserts are typically low-lying, flat, and covered with small boulders known as gibbers. The largest is Sturts Stony Desert which lies between Cooper Creek and the Diamantina River in northern South Australia. Like the sandy desert regions, the area's vegetation comprises low saltbush (genus *Atriplex*) and varieties of hardy spinifex grass.

Beyond these sparsely vegetated areas lie two vast desert regions characterised by scrub vegetation and tussock grasses. The scrub desert areas stretch from western Victoria and western New South Wales through South Australia, across the Nullarbor Plain and into Western Australia where they lie to the south of the Great Sandy, Gibson and Great Victoria deserts.

The vegetation of these areas includes extensive stands of low woodland mulga (*Acacia aneura*), vast areas of poor soils sparsely covered by grasses, and scattered areas of small myall, bluebush, saltbush and samphire trees. The land is marginal and hardly suitable for grazing, although it is not uncommon for large sheep stations to be established with the graziers relying on good seasons to produce enough grass to feed their animals.

There are very few tall trees in the desert. The name 'Nullarbor', for example, means 'no trees' in Latin. Although this is the case for a relatively small area of the Nullarbor Plain, it is true that there are no extensive stands of trees on the plain and that only isolated, scrubby trees are common.

The one notable exception is the ghost gum, sometimes known as the brittle or snappy gum, which will grow wherever there is any available water. This beautiful tree develops a large root system to ensure that it maximises its water intake.

The north-east limit of the desert reaches into Queensland's Gulf Country. In good wet seasons it is watered by the Diamantina—Cooper Creek river system which flows into Lake Eyre in South Australia. This is marginal land characterised by intermittent woodland areas of red gums, coolabahs and swamp box, and flat plains of saltbush. The periodic water, combined with bores which tap into the artesian basin lying hundreds of metres below the surface, sustain grasslands that have been used for both cattle and sheep grazing. There is now evidence that in the 19th century these marginal desert lands suffered from serious over-grazing. So extensive was the grazing that, by the end of that century, both Bourke and Wilcannia were active inland ports receiving wool from the sheep runs of northern New South Wales and western Queensland. For decades, Bourke's port was the only efficient way to transport wool to the coastal markets, and at its height in the late 1800s over 40 000 bales of wool were being shipped annually. The river transport continued until 1931.

One of the true idiosyncrasies of Australia's desert areas is the presence of 'lakes'. These are not conventional freshwater lakes. The unusual drainage patterns of western Queensland and central Australia have produced hundreds of saltwater lakes. In periods of drought they dry up and become little more than arid saltpans. However, during periods of good rainfall the lakes fill up and become havens for birdlife, with reeds, trees and grasses growing along the shoreline.

Australia's grey eucalypts

Australia is a land of gum trees, or grey eucalypts. They are an integral part of the country's identity; the scented grey-blue leaves and rugged trunks of gum trees are distinctly Australian. It has been estimated that Australia is home to around 500 species of gum or eucalypt. These vary from giant forests of karri in the south-western sectors of Western Australia to the smaller mallee eucalypts on the edges of the deserts.

Above: *Vast areas of inland Australia comprise flat, undifferentiated desert with hardy scrub and grasses surviving on rainfall that rarely rises above 250 millimetres per annum.*

What are the characteristics of this dominant tree? It commonly has visible oil glands on the leaves. This means that when crushed they give off a distinctive aroma. The flowers vary from white to yellow, orange, pink and red. Flowering is often irregular, occurring in some species every few years. The most common flowering season is late spring through to autumn.

The eucalypt is noted for its distinctive and widely variable bark. Ironbark varieties have tough, somewhat flaky bark. Candle bark has white to pink smooth bark which peels off in strips, and the stringy-barks and mahoganies are characterised as the name implies by stringy short fibres. There is a great diversity of colours, ranging from creamy timbers to deep red and brown.

Since the early 19th century the burgeoning timber industry, dependent on native growth forest, has been one of the country's major sources of income and employment. In all cases the development of the industry has followed a similar path. By the mid-19th century, timber cutters, leading lonely lives and working in extremely difficult terrain, had moved into areas along the coast where there were good stands of commercial timber.

Each region basically has the same history and evolution. In Western Australia, for example, logging has been an integral part of the economic history of the hinterland between Perth and Albany since the 1840s. The story is one of conflicting interests between exploitation and conservation. It has been about the growth of small, industry-specific timber towns, and about the difficulty of hauling the logs from the forests to the sawmills and from the sawmills to the coast.

Timber cutting in the area south of Perth started in the 1840s. It was a hard life and the government provided no assistance. In many instances it seemed the government was actively working against the interests of the timber workers. It refused to build railways and tried to regulate the industry by issuing licences to timber cutters. At the time there was little interest in, or infrastructure for, the development of exports, and the timber industry relied entirely on local sales. However, by 1874, overseas timber markets had been developed to a point where exports exceeded local production requirements. The development of export markets created an urgent need for ports, and the towns of Lockeville, Vasse, Karridale, Denmark, Jarrahdale and Collie all grew up to meet this demand.

By the 1880s the government had realised the size and importance of the industry. Its initial half-hearted attempts to control indiscriminate felling of trees

Above: This delicate beautiful bloom is produced by the red flowering gum.

had little impact. In the 1890s a railway line was built between Perth and Bridgetown and more coastal timber towns were established.

In 1895 the environmental issues were so worrying that the state's first Conservator of Forests was appointed. He tried to control the industry but failed due to political apathy, the power of the timber lobby and the fact that few people recognised the state's timber as a finite resource. It wasn't until 1916 that another Conservator of Forests was appointed. The second Conservator drafted legislation designed to protect the state's forests and the timber industry. The legislation included the planting of pine trees to meet the state's softwood requirements, the dedication of state forests and strictly administered regeneration regimes. So successful was the legislation that the number of sawmills tripled in one year. This initial enthusiasm was short-lived; the Depression and World War II had negative effects. It was not until after the war that the industry started to recover. Improvements in hauling logs, modern timber-felling techniques, and an increased need for plywoods and woodchips saw both total production and total exports increase dramatically.

Today, Western Australia has nearly 2 million hectares of forest under state control; the aim is to balance development with conservation. The major issue is to meet the requirements of both the timber industry and environmentalists. Where everyone does agree is that the eucalypt forests are one of the country's most critical natural resources.

Above: To protect themselves from the harshness of the environment, rural Australians designed houses with wide verandahs to provide ample shade.

The world of the mallee plains

'Mallee' is an Aboriginal word whose original meaning is unknown and which has been used to describe a range of small to medium-sized eucalypts which grow in semi-arid areas in south-eastern, South and Western Australia.

The largest single area of these eucalypts is known as the Mallee District, and covers some 44 000 square kilometres of western Victoria from the South Australian border to the Murray River and south to Kerang and Birchip. The centrepieces of this area are the Little Desert National Park, the Wyperfield National Park (which contains the Big Desert Wilderness Park) and the Murray—Sunset National Park.

The Mallee District is marginal country and has never been seen as having great agricultural potential. It is known that, before European settlement, small numbers of Aborigines lived in the area. They dug wells for water, found crustaceans in the Murray River and survived by hunting the sparse animal population.

The first Europeans to explore western Victoria travelled through the district in the 1830s—Charles Sturt arrived in 1830, Thomas Mitchell in 1836, Edward Eyre in 1838 and John Gould in 1839—and, without exception, described the area as difficult and forbidding. What they were confronted with was poor rainfall—between 130 and 380 milli-

metres a year—and soils deprived of vital minerals. What they failed to appreciate was that the mallee had a subtle and fascinating ecology with a rich diversity of flowering plants and unusual fauna, including the mallee kangaroo and the ring-necked parrot, as well as the mallee fowl, or lowan, which builds a mound of sand and debris in which its eggs are incubated.

As the graziers herded cattle and sheep westward, people started to clear the mallee. It was a relatively easy process, as the trees were small and could be easily burnt. What the land clearers failed to appreciate was that the complex mallee roots were necessary to hold the soil together. The clearance of the mallee for wheat growing was only effective until times of drought when dry winds blew the loose soil away.

As conservationists and environmentalists became interested in the ecology of the mallee, there was a move to have the government isolate the areas concerned and declare them national parks. This occurred in western Victoria where large tracts of mallee were set aside to protect its fauna and flora.

The Little Desert National Park has extensive stands of yellow mallee and flowering ti-trees, and although this land was once used for grazing, it was set aside specifically to protect the habitat of the mallee fowl.

Large areas of the Wyperfield National Park had been settled by 1847. Set aside as a park in 1909, the area has rich and diverse fauna and flora with over 300 plant species and 180 bird species, including the mallee fowl.

There are also mallee conservation parks in New South Wales (particularly around West Wyalong), in Western Australia (the Nuytsland Nature Reserve) and in both eastern and western South Australia. None of the areas has ever been ideal for grazing, and as the greed of the 19th century has given way to a rational and sympathetic understanding of the mallee's ecology they have been turned into parks for the preservation of fauna and flora.

Grasses and heathland

Australia's heathlands, which consist of areas covered with xerophytic shrubs, exist in eastern Australia, small areas of South Australia and the south-western corner of Western Australia. Further south, similar heathland is found in the Grampians in Victoria, along the northern and southern shores of Bass Strait, and in the Coorong region of the southern parts of South Australia.

In all cases the heathland has resisted grazing and development. Basically inhospitable, the soils are poor, and the plants are characteristically hardy, with small sharp leaves and wiry stems. Large

Above: *The mallee area is marginal country which, in good seasons, can sustain sheep and wheat. The term 'mallee' is used to describe a range of small- to medium-sized eucalypts which grow in semi-arid areas in south-eastern Australia, South Australia and Western Australia.*

Above: *Koalas sleep for much of the day supported in the forks of gum trees.*

stands of eucalypts are uncommon in the heathlands. Instead, the ground is covered by small ground shrubs which belong predominantly to the *Banksia*, *Melaleuca*, *Acacia* and *Hakea* genera. At certain times of the year these hardy, unattractive plants burst into flower.

One truly remarkable heathland is that of south-western Western Australia. Known as the greatest wildflower display on the continent, the heathlands support up to 12 000 species and, in spring, tens of thousands of hectares burst into bloom. This diversity is equal to the rainforests of the Amazon basin. The terrain is flat and uninviting, and in areas like Kalbarri National Park the soil is poor, rocky and sandy; yet between August and October over 200 000 hectares become a vast carpet of wildflowers.

The landscape is either flat or slightly undulating, the soil infertile and sandy. In spite of these conditions, the area contains all of the world's dryandras, most of its species of banksia and more than half of its sundews (*Drosera*).

ANIMAL DIVERSITY

In the beginning

The antiquity of the Australian landmass has left evidence that some sort of primordial life form existed in Western Australia around 3800 million years ago. Add to this evidence of perfectly formed cells from rocks in the MacDonnell Ranges which are around 900 million years old and it is clear that human settlement accounts for little more than a millisecond on the continent's biological and botanical clock.

This extraordinary longevity has allowed many species unique to the continent to develop, adapt and survive. One of the widely accepted reasons for Australia's unique faunal diversity has been the absence of seriously competitive predators. However, it is inaccurate to suggest that the continent has no predators. It has had predators ranging from dingoes through crocodiles and goannas to the Tasmanian tiger (*Thylocinus cynocephalus*), Tasmanian

wolf (*Thylacinus cynocephalus*), marsupial lion (*Thylacoleo carnifex*) and Tasmanian devil (*Sarcophilis harrisii*); and, in recent times, many benign species have been endangered, and in some cases made extinct, by a rapidly increasing population of carnivorous feral dogs and cats.

There is evidence, particularly in far western Queensland, of the presence of dinosaurs. Situated 110 kilometres from Winton, The Lark Quarry Environmental Park, is famous for its Dinosaur Stampede which offers an interesting fossilised insight into life some 95 million years ago. This is the largest group of footprints (some 1200) of running dinosaurs uncovered anywhere in the world. Three species of dinosaur were responsible for the tracks—a large flesh-eating carnosaur and many small coelurosaurs and ornithopods.

As far as can be determined, there were some 250 species of furred animal and 650 species of bird spread across the continent in 1788. Over millions of years these animals had modified themselves to survive in the harsh conditions produced by infertile soils, poor vegetation, and intermittent droughts and floods. Their modified reproductive cycles, their ability to use only limited supplies of protein and their efficiency in making their young self-sufficient had all contributed to species which, in many instances, were dramatically different from related species which had evolved on other continents.

There is evidence that a wide range of Australian animals—particularly mammals such as the koala, wombat and kangaroo, as well as lizards and birds—reproduce sparingly. Over millions of years the koala has developed into a highly efficient energy saver, with a reduced brain (apparently to conserve energy) and a diet which is based entirely on eucalypt leaves. The koala has become so selective in its eating habits that it relies on specific leaves, which it carefully chooses for their high nutrients, and it conserves its energy so that it needs to eat infrequently. Similarly, the wombat preserves energy by being the only large herbivorous mammal on earth to live in a burrow.

Although an island continent, and therefore less vulnerable to animal migration, Australia has still been affected by animals carried by birds and the wind, and by objects floating across from the Indonesian archipelago. Since the arrival of humans, non-native animals have dramatically affected the continuing existence of a number of species. There is, for example, evidence that the arrival of dingoes led to the extinction of the flightless Tasmanian native hen on the continental mainland.

Marsupials

Available evidence suggests that the first marsupials arrived in Australia around 100 million years ago. No one knows why these marsupials (creatures which have not developed placental birth) survived and prospered in such diversity. The first arrivals, which seem to have been tree-climbing creatures (the ancestors of modern-day possums), probably travelled from the Asian mainland.

It is likely that most modern-day marsupials—possums, wombats, kangaroos, wallabies, echidnas and gliders—evolved from this single common source. There is evidence that some of these species were remarkably successful. At one point, giant wombats (reputedly the size of a small hippopotamus) and kangaroos over 3 metres tall inhabited the country.

Australia's isolation from other continents, and its relative lack of predators, provided the marsupials with an environment in which they prospered. It is significant that since the arrival of Europeans at least six species of marsupial have become extinct.

It is a remarkable testament to their resilience that many of the other species of marsupial have survived. Hundreds of thousands of wombats, for example, were slaughtered by angry farmers who found that the creature's penchant for burrowing was destroying their rabbit-proof fencing.

Similarly, in the late 19th century, koalas were killed for their skins. The industry in koala skins started around 1890. By 1919 it had grown to such a level that an estimated 1 million koalas were killed during that year. The trade was finally halted in 1928. However, over half a million koalas were killed during the 1927 season.

The figures for kangaroos are equally disturbing. Since earliest times, farmers and graziers have killed kangaroos because they have been the most visible competitors for grazing lands.

Kangaroos are still widely perceived as pests and vermin by graziers in marginal areas. Consequently, professional kangaroo hunters operate in areas of the country like western Queensland where

they kill to a government-controlled quota system. The skins are used for handbags and the meat supports an active domestic pet food industry.

Today there are 16 defined families of marsupials, of which 13 exist only in Australia. The other three families, all varieties of opossum, are found in the Americas. The range of marsupials in Australia includes over 60 species of kangaroo (family Macropodidae), the koala (family Phascolarctidae), three species of wombat (family Vombatidae), 22 species of gliders and ring-tailed possums (family Petauridae), 11 species of brush-tailed possum and cuscus (family Phalangeridae), seven species of pygmy phalangers (family Burramyidae), 18 species of bandicoot which comprise two distinct families —Thylacomyidae and Peramelidae—a solitary species of marsupial mole (*Notoryctes typhlops*), and the Dasyuridae family which includes all the carnivorous and insectivorous marsupials ranging from quolls to dunnarts, phascogales, numbats, banded ant-eaters and the Tasmanian devil.

Reptiles

Australia's native reptiles range from huge crocodiles to a bewildering range of lizards and includes a number of tortoises and turtles as well as some of the world's largest and most deadly snakes.

Long after the dinosaurs had disappeared, the continent had an impressive array of savage and dangerous reptiles. Before the arrival of humans Australia was home to a species of 3-metre-long, land-based crocodile (*Quinkana fortirostrum*) and huge goanna (*Megalania prisca*), both of which weighed over 200 kilograms and fed off marsupials. As well, there was a species of large python (*Wonambi narracoortensis*) living in southern Australia which grew to over 6 metres in length and weighed over 100 kilograms.

Today the continent is known for its diversity of reptiles. The larger reptiles include more than five species of goanna weighing over 5 kilograms, five species of large python and two species of crocodile (the freshwater and saltwater). The saltwater, or estuarine, crocodile (*Crocodylus porosus*) is the world's

Above: *The deadly saltwater, or estuarine, crocodile inhabits the rivers and ocean shallows of northern Queensland, the Northern Territory and northern Western Australia.*

Top: *The kookaburra is famous for its laughing call as well as its ability to catch and kill snakes and lizards.*

Bottom: *Rainbow lorikeets are noisy birds, commonly travelling in screeching and chattering flocks.*

largest living reptile, growing to a length of around 6 metres. It lives in mangroves, coastal swamp areas and river mouths in far north Queensland, the Northern Territory and the Kimberley region of Western Australia. Although its diet is predominantly fish, turtles and birds, it has been known to attack and kill large land animals as well as humans.

The freshwater, or Johnston's, crocodile (*Crocodylus johnstoni*) is a much smaller creature than the saltwater species, growing to a length of 2 metres. Although not dangerous to humans, it has been known to attack when provoked. It lives on fish, small reptiles and mammals it may catch on the riverbanks. Unique to northern Australia, it is now a protected species.

Approximately 160 different snakes, many of which are extremely poisonous, inhabit Australia and its coastal waters.

Australia has 10 species of python, the largest being the rock python which has been known to grow to 8.5 metres. It is common in central and northern Queensland, living off small mammals and birds which it crushes and swallows.

By contrast, the continent's smallest snakes belong to the blind or worm snake family (Typhlopidae). These snakes do not exist in Tasmania. There are around 20 species on the mainland, all of which are non-venomous.

Although 70 per cent of Australia's snakes are venomous, only eight can be fairly described as dangerous. The most famous of these are the taipan, the family of tiger snakes, the black snake, death adder and copperhead, the family of brown snakes, the fierce snake— sometimes known as the giant brown snake (*Parademansia microlepidota*) and reputed to be the most venomous—and the rough-scaled snake, which has been known to kill people.

Of the other reptiles commonly found in Australia there are many geckos, a range of bearded dragon lizards, nearly 20 species of fast monitor lizard (sometimes known as the goanna), skinks, river and ocean turtles, sea snakes and the remarkable thorny devil lizard.

There is scientific evidence from central Australia that up to 47 different lizard species have been found in single sand dunes, and it is known that there are more reptiles in Australia's desert regions than exist in any other single environment on earth.

Birdlife

There is some dispute as to how many different species of bird inhabit Australia. In 1926, 707 species were officially listed. This was later reduced to 651 and then increased to around 720. The problem lies in the migratory nature of many birds and the difficulty in recording rare and nocturnal species.

Early explorers and settlers were amazed by some of the continent's unique species. It is known, for example, that the Dutch settlers in Batavia (the former name of Jakarta in Java) were

fascinated by the black swans which Willem de Vlamingh caught near the Swan River, and the British were suitably awed by the lyrebird sent to London by Governor John Hunter.

The early settlers showed immense interest in such unusual species as the bellbird, the cockatoo, the emu and the kookaburra. They were equally impressed by the exquisitely coloured parrots and lorikeets which were found in the rainforests near Sydney.

The migratory nature of birds means that most of the species unique to the Australian continent are ground birds incapable of flying long distances. This group of birds includes two species of lyrebird, the whipbird, the pilot bird, the mallee fowl, the wedgebill, the quail thrush, two species of scrub bird, the bristle bird, as well as the Spinifex bird and the grass wren.

Of these birds the most ancient is the pilot bird (genus *Pycnoptilus*), a relative of an extinct species that inhabited the continent during the Pleistocene era.

The aptly named superb lyrebird (*Menura novaehollandiae*) and the less well-known Prince Albert lyrebird (*Menura alberti*) are ground birds famous for their mimicry. The habitat of the superb lyrebird stretches through the Great Dividing Range from Melbourne as far north as southern Queensland; the Prince Albert lyrebird is restricted to the forests near the New South Wales—Queensland border. The lyrebird is shy, but its display and 'dance'—associated with mating and breeding—are particularly impressive.

The two species of ground-dwelling scrub bird (genus *Atrichornis*) are closely related to the lyrebird. One lives in the woodlands of the south-western part of Western Australia, while the other lives in south-eastern Queensland. Living in similar habitats are the two species of bristle bird (genus *Dasyornis*) which rarely fly, preferring to run through the undergrowth and build dome-shaped nests.

The two whipbirds (genus *Psophodes*) seem to be unconnected to any other species of bird and are considered uniquely Australian. Known as the common or coachwhip bird (*Psophodes olivaceus*) and the eastern whipbird

Above: *Aborigines in the Northern Territory dressed for a corroboree in the early 20th century. Similar celebrations are still held today.*

(*Psophodes nigrogularis*), they are small and live in dense undergrowth, feed on insects, and are famous along the Great Dividing Range from southern Victoria to northern Queensland because of their distinctive call which sounds like a whip being cracked.

Similar in size and shape to the whipbird is the wedgebill (*Sphenostroma cristatum*), a small brown thrush which lives in bushes, low trees and on the ground in the Australian interior. The grass wrens (there are probably 10 in the species) are another uniquely Australian bird group which, like the wedgebill, live in arid areas and, although capable of flying, prefer to travel along the ground. They tend to live in tussocks of porcupine grass.

Other birds which, while not being uniquely Australian are integral to the excitement and beauty of the bush, are the ubiquitous magpies and crows, the kookaburra, or kingfisher, with its distinctive mocking laughter, the emus which inhabit the dry inland areas, and the spectacularly beautiful parrots, cockatoos, rosellas, galahs and lorikeets. Few sights in Australia are more impressive than a group of brightly coloured king parrots darting through the bush.

Nearly one-third of the country's bird species are nomadic and are capable of responding rapidly to changing ecological circumstances.

Introduced fauna

The first known introduced species was the dingo, which was brought to Australia around 3500 years ago. While there is some dispute about this date, it is known that the dingo arrived after Tasmania had been cut off from the mainland by the rise in sea level. It is also known that, like most introduced species, the dingo wreaked havoc on those species ill-equipped to deal with its predatory hunting techniques. Both the Tasmanian devil and the now-extinct Tasmanian tiger once existed on the mainland. They were both on the mainland long before the Europeans arrived.

With the arrival of the Europeans the continent's native fauna was drastically altered by the introduction of species which not only prospered but which competed with, and in many cases lived off, the native species.

The arrival of rabbits, foxes, goats and pigs, birds such as the sparrow, starling and blackbird, a number of species of deer and, especially, the domestic cat and dog (both of which went feral) all impacted on the environment. The greatest environmental damage was undoubtedly caused by introduced grazing animals—sheep and cattle—which consumed vast grasslands, did great damage with their hoofed feet, and competed for pasture with herbivores such as the kangaroo and wallaby.

HISTORY AND GOVERNMENT

The Arrival of Aborigines

In recent times, attempts to determine precisely when the first Aborigines arrived in Australia have been the subject of considerable debate. For many years, largely as the result of the work of the American anthropologist Joseph Birdsell during the 1930s, there was a belief that the continent had experienced three major periods of Aboriginal immigration. Birdsell put forward the 'trihybrid' theory in an attempt to explain the perception that there were three distinctly different groups of Aborigines. One group, he claimed, could be found in north Queensland and Tasmania, another group in south-eastern Australia and a third group around the Gulf of Carpentaria. Birdsell claimed that these groups had started to arrive around 30 000 years ago and completed their emigration around 10 000 years ago.

A 'two migration' theory enjoyed popularity during the 19th century. This theory argued that there were so many differences between Tasmanian and mainland Aborigines that they must have had separate origins. It argued that the two groups were physically different, and that the Tasmanians did not use such culturally defining tools as the boomerang and spear thrower. There were also distinct dietary differences. The theory was rejected when it was established that the physical separation of Tasmania and the Australian mainland only occurred 12 000 years ago.

Due to lack of hard evidence, neither of these theories can be completely discounted although it is quite likely that all modern-day Australian Aborigines are descendants of a single migration which occurred sometime between 40 000 and 55 000 years ago. The evidence used to support the theory of single migration includes clear links between all Aboriginal languages currently spoken in Australia and the fact that there is no clear archaeological evidence of two separate cultures.

Dispersal of Aboriginal culture

It is clear that the first Aborigines, whenever they arrived, must have come by sea as Asia and Australia have not been connected for many millions of years. Their journey must have been epic. Travelling at least 50 kilometres across unknown waters, probably in a raft made from bark or from a log, must have been extraordinarily dangerous.

Above: *Most aborigines live in urban environments. However, in the outback many communities successfully combine modern and traditional lifestyles.*

The first definite evidence of human occupation of Australia can be carbon dated to 35 000—40 000 years ago. It is significant that these ancient camps, with their food and charcoal remnants from fires, have all been found on the edges of inland lakes in far western New South Wales. As yet, no evidence has come to light of early human settlement around the northern coastline of the continent. This does not mean that settlement did not occur in these regions. In fact, it has been suggested that the first Aborigines could have arrived as early as 60 000 years ago, although a figure around 55 000 years ago seems more likely. It is argued that it took close to 10 000 years for the Aborigines to move across the continent.

So what early evidence do we have of Aborigines on the Australian continent? The most ancient skeletons were discovered around Lake Mungo in western New South Wales in the 1970s. The first skeleton found was that of a woman who had been cremated. The fact that her body had been burnt suggested some form of religious ritual (if this is correct, the Aborigines had a spiritual and religious system long before any other human society) and allowed for relatively accurate carbon dating of the remains. According to the initial dating, she had died around 38 000 years ago. This was later reduced to around 35 000 years ago.

Four years later the skeleton of a man who lived around 32 000 years ago was found in the Lake Mungo area. In the 1980s, caves in Western Australia and Tasmania revealed the presence of humans dating back to the same period.

Most of what is known about the Aborigines who lived on the mainland is considered guesswork based on small amounts of evidence. It does seem likely that the continent's earliest inhabitants possessed large stone axes and had developed a sophisticated language. They almost certainly lived in small, economically viable groups, much as the Aborigines do today. They had no domesticated animals, and there is no evidence that they planted seeds. Their shelters were probably no more than simple, easily erected structures.

One of the most significant events in the history of the Aboriginal people was the rise in sea level which separated the Tasmanian Aborigines from those on the mainland. It was still possible to walk from southern Victoria to Tasmania as recently as 13 000 years ago. When the waters rose, the Tasmanian, Kangaroo Island and Flinders Island Aborigines were isolated.

The Tasmanians evolved a number of unique qualities in a short period of time. By the time the Europeans had arrived they had dispensed with any form of clothing, preferring to use animal fat to protect themselves from the cold. They had no means of making fire, and relied on fire generated naturally as a source of fuel. This latter situation meant that when their fires went out, they had to eat raw meat until they made contact with another group which had managed to keep a fire alight. It was a cultural imperative that fire had to be given to anyone who requested it.

They did not eat fish. In spite of the rich supplies surrounding the island they rejected the fish offered by both French and British explorers, expressing horror that anyone would want to eat it. The Tasmanians did not have boomerangs or spear throwers, nor did they make stone axes or use bone to make their tools.

What is remarkable about these cultural variations is that they evolved rapidly. Most of the artefacts absent from Tasmanian Aboriginal society in the late 18th century had existed as recently as 7000 years before. There is ample evidence that 3500 years ago, Tasmanian Aborigines used bone tools, including sophisticated needles which they used to sew animal skins together. There is also evidence that, at that time, they were eating fish and using boomerangs and spear throwers.

It is not clear how or why the first Tasmanians 'lost' aspects of their social and cultural life. The most plausible explanation for this social and cultural decline is that a combination of isolation and a small population meant that vital skills were held by small numbers of people. If those people were killed or died before they could pass on the skill, then it was lost.

Perhaps the lesson to be learnt from the Tasmanian experience is that pre-European Aboriginal life on the Australian continent was complex, subtle and diverse. Most early European settlers, when they bothered to think about or comprehend Aboriginal society, tended to see it as a single, coherent whole and refused to understand that 40 000 years had allowed for the evolution of social organisations uniquely designed to deal with different environments and differing needs.

There is now considerable evidence that, with the exception of the communities which lived along the Murray River, Aboriginal tribal groups tended to number around 500 people. These groups adapted to their local regions and modified their behaviour when their region changed. Thus the Aborigines in Arnhem Land used boomerangs 3 millennia ago but stopped using them when the vegetation became too dense. Similarly, some groups used dingoes for hunting but, as a general principle, they used the dogs mostly for warmth at night. Some groups on the coast relied on shellfish for their staple diet, while groups living away from the coast ate small animals, seeds and vegetables according to what was available.

In his book *The Future Eaters*, Dr Timothy Flannery notes that the greatest factor determining Aboriginal lifestyle was the impact of El Niño, which militated against agriculture and forced them into a nomadic existence.

Estimates of the Aboriginal population prior to the arrival of the first settlers in 1788 vary widely. The best estimate is somewhere between 300 000 and 600 000. What is remarkable is that there were at least 250 different language groups and that, in spite of this apparent cultural diversity, these groups were loosely interconnected. Their 'songlines', as the Aborigines' trade and spiritual routes are sometimes called, were spread right across the continent. The evidence of these connections includes the discovery of pearl shells from Broome as far south as Victoria as well as evidence of stone quarried in northern Queensland found on the edge of the Nullarbor.

Above: *Cape York is the most northerly point on Australia's east coast. From earliest times, Indonesian traders plied the narrow Torres Strait between Cape York and New Guinea.*

The arrival of traders and fishers

The economic forces and navigational skills which brought the Aborigines to the Australian mainland did not vanish. There is evidence, from earliest times, that traders and fishers from the islands of the Indonesian archipelago continued to make the short journey across to Arnhem Land, and that the narrow Torres Strait between Cape York and New Guinea was regularly crossed.

Most of the people who made the journey were the seafaring Macassans from the island of Sulawesi. They traded throughout the Indonesian archipelago.

Their journeys to northern Australia were fishing expeditions in search of the *bêche-de-mer*, or sea urchin, which they dried and exported to mainland China.

Remarkably, only a month before Captain Arthur Phillip arrived in Botany Bay, a larger fleet set sail from Macassar for Arnhem Land where the crew collected *bêche-de-mer* and tortoise shells. This fleet was just one of many regular expeditions to northern Australia.

The Macassans left evidence of their presence. Along the continent's northern coast there are still stone fireplaces built to boil the *bêche-de-mer*. Archaeologists

EUROPEAN VOYAGES OF DISCOVERY

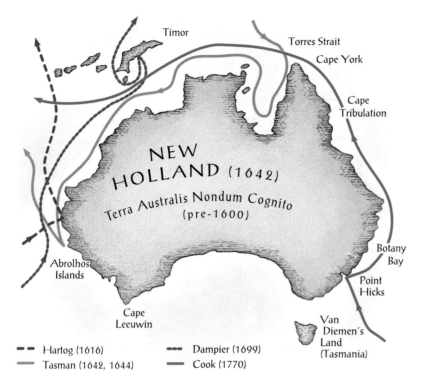

Legend:
- - - Hartog (1616)
—— Tasman (1642, 1644)
••• Dampier (1699)
—— Cook (1770)

have also found shards of clay pots and fishing hooks. While most of the activity started in the 16th century, there is evidence that the Macassans were coming to the coast much earlier. Today, Macassans and fishers from the Indonesian archipelago still stray into Australian waters.

Their impact on Aboriginal society has been enormous. They had enough regular contact with local communities to have influenced the language. In Arnhem Land, Aborigines referred to Europeans as *balanda*, an Indonesian word for the Dutch, long before the arrival of European explorers.

There is also strong evidence that sexual relations existed between the Macassan sailors and the local Aborigine population. The Macassans might have brought Dutch goods to the coast, including axes, knives and glassware.

Similarly, the contact between Cape York and the coastal regions of Papua New Guinea has been well documented. It is known that some Torres Strait Islanders speak a language from Papua and that there are some groups along the Papuan coast that speak a distinct Aboriginal language. It is also recognised that some Torres Strait Islanders and Cape York Aborigines have distinctive Melanesian physical features.

So powerful were the links across the Torres Strait that there is evidence of shared myths and belief systems, as well as symbols of religious expression including the use of body painting, masks, and items woven from grass.

The first coastal explorers

As early as the 5th century BC the Greeks seemed to know of the existence of a large landmass south of Asia.

There is now considerable evidence that the first non-Aborigines and non-island traders to reach Australia were the Chinese. They were accomplished seafarers and, as early as AD860, they were regularly travelling around the coasts of Asia and the Indian subcontinent and trading along the east coast of Africa. The theory that the Chinese were the first to discover Australia gained credibility when a Chinese soapstone carving of a man on a horse, dating from the early 1400s, was found near the modern-day site of Darwin in 1879.

It is known that Chinese explorers had reached Timor by the 15th century. Add to this the fact that Macassan traders were selling *bêche-de-mer* caught in Australian waters to the Chinese by the 16th century and it is hard to believe that the Chinese did not reach, and possibly explore, northern Australia.

Early European explorers

The first Europeans to reach Australia were the Portuguese. By 1418 they had reached the Canary Islands in the Atlantic, and by the mid-15th century they had discovered the Azores and reached Guinea on the west coast of Africa. They rounded the Cape of Good Hope in 1487 and by 1500 had entered the Indian Ocean. They reached Ceylon (Sri Lanka) in 1506 and were establishing trading posts in the East Indies in 1510–11. By 1520 they had reached as far east as Timor.

It seems likely that the Portuguese reached the Australian mainland at around this time. However, any evidence of this is difficult and contradictory. There is no known journal or ship's log which definitely describes a sighting of the Australian coast. The evidence available relies on a number of maps produced in France between 1530 and 1560. These maps, produced by cartographers in the French port of Dieppe, depict a huge south land which they name 'Java la Grande'. This landmass had been copied from Portuguese maps and roughly approximated the size of the Australian continent.

This fascination with a great southern continent, which cartographers named 'Terra Australis Nondum Cognito', led the Portuguese viceroy at Goa on the west coast of India to send an expedition east in 1521. They did not reach the continent. In 1568 the viceroy of Peru, convinced of the existence of a land of great wealth, sent Pedro de Quiros and Luis Vaez de Torres west to seek the great south land. They left Peru in three vessels on 21 December 1605. Eventually Torres reached the narrow straits between Australia and Papua New Guinea which are now named after him. For two months he sailed along the southern coast of Papua New Guinea. In spite of its importance, Torres's discovery was largely ignored and no further Portuguese exploration was undertaken.

The first confirmed sightings of the Australian continent occurred in the early 17th century by Dutch merchants trying to expand their sphere of influence beyond the East Indies. Willem Janssen sailed the *Duyfken* east from Batavia to explore the easternmost islands of the East Indies archipelago. He reached the west coast of Cape York in 1606 and explored between latitudes 11°S and 14°S. When he returned, his discovery was noted but its significance was largely ignored.

Later, the Dutch, now well established in the East Indies, decided to take a more southerly route across the Indian Ocean. Previously they had followed the coast of Africa north, then sailed directly east to Sumatra. In 1610, however, Henderik Brouwer discovered that the best route from the Cape of Good Hope to Batavia was via the Roaring Forties. He headed directly eastward from the Cape for approximately 5300 kilometres before turning north towards Java. However, unable to accurately calculate distance and wind speed, the discovery of Western Australia was inevitable as soon as a Dutch ship overshot its mark and encountered the coast.

Six years later, Dirk Hartog sailed too far and landed at Cape Inscription on 26 October 1616. It was here that Hartog left an inscribed pewter plate. It is firm evidence of the first European landing on mainland Australia.

In 1697, another Dutch sailor, Willem de Vlamingh, reached the island and, finding Hartog's pewter plate still in its original position (although badly weathered), he removed it and replaced it with another plate. The original was returned to Holland where it is still kept in the Rijksmuseum in Amsterdam.

In 1818 the French explorer Louis de Freycinet, while exploring the coast, came across de Vlamingh's plate and removed it to France. The plate was eventually returned to Australia in 1947 and is currently housed in the Maritime Museum in Fremantle.

Hartog was followed in May 1618 by Claeszoon van Hillegom in the *Zeewolf*. A

few months later, in July, Jacobszoon sailed up the coast in the *Mauritius* and the following year the Abrolhos Islands were sighted and reported by Frederick Houtman. Two years later the Houtman Abrolhos reefs claimed their first known victim, the *Batavia*. Once the *Batavia* had struck Morning Reef near Traitors Island at the eastern end of the Wallabi archipelago, Captain Francisco Pelsaert took the ship's boat and with 47 of the survivors sailed up the coast to Batavia (a remarkable feat), while the mutinous Jeronimus Cornelisz terrorised the

remaining survivors and eventually murdered 125 of them. The Houtman Abrolhos reefs have the dubious distinction of being the first white settlement in Australia. This first settlement included two forts (which can still be seen today), was the site of a massacre and, when Pelsaert returned, was the scene of horrendous punishments.

As a consequence of these explorations the governor-general of Batavia, Anthonie van Diemen, decided to send an expedition to explore the land to the south of Java. On 14 August 1642, Abel

Above: *The coastline near Carnarvon in Western Australia is lonely, dry and inhospitable.*

Tasman, leading an expedition which comprised the ships *Heemskirk* and *Zeehaen*, sailed from Batavia. On 24 November, Tasman sighted an island which he named Van Diemen's Land (today known as Tasmania). He sailed around the island's south coast and north to Storm Bay. A small group, who had been sent ashore, heard voices, but did not see anybody. Noting steps cut nearly 2 metres apart on the side of a tree, they assumed that the island was inhabited by giants. Instead of sailing north—which would have resulted in the discovery of eastern Australia—Tasman sailed east into the Pacific, discovering New Zealand and the group of islands which James Cook subsequently named the Friendly Islands.

William Dampier was the first British sailor to reach Australia. His successful journals of his journey through the Antipodes—*A New Voyage Round the World* and *A Voyage to New Holland*—captured the imagination of the British public as Australia was portrayed as a harsh country full of barbarians. The Britain were to show little interest in New Holland for the next 70 years.

THE VOYAGE OF THE HMS BARK *ENDEAVOUR*

22 August 1770
Cape York

Cape Flattery
Cooktown
Cape Tribulation

NEW HOLLAND

Cape Morton

Point Danger

Botany Bay

Point Hicks
19 April 1770

NEW ZEALAND

Above: *Captain James Cook was the first European explorer to sight and explore the coast of eastern Australia.*

Cook's voyage up the coast

The issue which brought Captain James Cook to the east coast of Australia was astronomy. On 15 February 1768 the Royal Society in London suggested to its patron, King George III, that the transit of Venus should be observed from various points around the world. The argument was that Venus would eclipse the sun on 3 June 1769 and this event would allow astronomers to accurately measure the distance between the earth and the sun. The Royal Society suggested that the transit should be observed from three points around the globe—one in Scandinavia, one in Canada and one in the South Pacific.

King George III was interested in the project, as were British officials who, knowing that there was an undiscovered land in the southern Pacific, were eager to find it and add it to their growing empire. They agreed to provide £4000 to finance the venture. A 368-ton collier named the *Earl of Pembroke* was purchased and promptly renamed the *Endeavour*. On 25 May 1768, James Cook was commissioned as a lieutenant in the British Navy and two days

later he was given command of the *Endeavour*. On 26 August 1768 the *Endeavour* with 94 people aboard sailed from Plymouth, crossing the Atlantic to Rio de Janeiro.

By 13 April 1769 it had reached Tahiti where, on 3 June, the transit of Venus was observed. It was off the coast of Tahiti that Cook opened a sealed document, giving him instructions for the rest of his voyage. The Lords of the British Admiralty instructed him to proceed southward until he came across the great southern land and to:

> ... observe the Genius, Temper, Disposition and Number of the Natives, if there be any, and endeavour by all proper means to cultivate a Friendship and Alliance with them, making them presents of such Trifles as they may Value, inviting them to Traffick, and Shewing them every kind of Civility. You are also with the consent of the Natives to take possession of the Convenient Situations in the Country in the Name of the King of Great Britain; or, if you find the Country uninhabited take Possession for His Majesty by setting up Proper Marks and Inscriptions, as first discoverers and possessors.

The *Endeavour* left Tahiti on 13 July and headed due west in search of the southern continent. After nearly 11 weeks at sea, during which time Cook and his crew examined the Society Islands and sailed west accompanied by sharks and porpoises, the vessel arrived at New Zealand. For six months they circumnavigated and mapped New Zealand's north and south islands.

By March 1770, Cook decided to head home to England. An original plan to sail south to Van Diemen's Land and then to the Cape of Good Hope was abandoned because of the threat of the oncoming winter winds in the southern oceans. Instead, Cook decided to head further north and it was this decision which resulted, at dawn on 19 April 1770, in Zachary Hicks sighting the east coast of Australia at a place now known as Point Hicks.

From the moment Cook sighted Australia he must have been aware that it was inhabited. It was clear that the land was fertile, and the smoke from campfires was evident as the *Endeavour* made its way up the coast. He saw ample evidence of Aboriginal settlement and, intriguingly, he admired their lifestyle. He described them as follows in his journal:

> From what I have said of the Natives of New-Holland they may appear to some to be the most wretched people upon Earth, but in reality they are far more happier than we Europeans; being wholly unacquainted not only with the superfluous but the necessary Conveniences so much sought after in Europe, they are happy in not knowing the use of them. They live in a Tranquillity which is not disturb'd by the Inequality of Condition: The Earth and the sea of their own accord furnishes them with all things necessary for life.

Yet, after spending two months at the present site of Cooktown after his ship was damaged on the Great Barrier Reef at Cape Tribulation, he sailed north and

Above: *After holing the* Endeavour *at Cape Tribulation, Captain Cook moored at the site of Cooktown in far north Queensland for six weeks. A statue of the great navigator celebrates this first, temporary European settlement.*

Above: *A perfect replica of Captain Cook's HM Bark* Endeavour *was built to celebrate the Bicentenary in 1988.*

on 22 August 1770 arrived at Possession Island where he claimed the entire east coast of Australia and named it 'New South Wales'.

All the evidence pointed towards the continent being occupied. So, why did Cook claim possession of the east coast? One of the most vexing questions about the creation of modern Australia centres on the concept of *terra nullius* and the attitude the British had towards unsettled lands at the end of the 18th century. The most likely explanation is a mixture of pragmatism and a dubious legal principle. There is little doubt that Cook's claim was an attempt to annex land which the British feared would fall into French hands.

It took only 18 years for them to decide that it would be a suitable place for a convict colony and to send the refuse of their penal system to Botany Bay in an attempt to clear the overcrowded prisons of Britain.

The first settlers

On 13 May 1787 a fleet of 11 vessels left the Isle of Wight and sailed into the English Channel. They were bound for Botany Bay to establish a penal colony. The fleet consisted of five transport ships—the *Alexander*, *Scarborough*,

Charlotte, *Lady Penrhyn* and *Friendship* —which were commissioned to carry the convicts. There were also four storeships —the *Fishbourne*, *Golden Grove*, *Borrowdale* and *Prince of Wales*—which had been commissioned to carry two years' provisions and the equipment necessary for building houses and quarters as well as establishing crops and vegetable gardens. The flagship of the fleet was the 520-ton HMS *Sirius* which was accompanied by a small brig, the HMS *Supply*.

The ships sailed via Tenerife in the Canary Islands and Rio de Janeiro in Brazil. They then crossed the Atlantic, took on supplies at the Cape of Good Hope and, on 12 November 1787, sailed on the Roaring Forties towards Australia. They arrived at Botany Bay on the night of 19 January 1788.

Governor Arthur Phillip was soon to determine that Botany Bay, which had been recommended by Cook for its good soils and deep grasses, was an unsuitable site. He was confronted with a major problem. The voyage from England had been predicated on Botany Bay being a suitable site for a penal colony. After eight months at sea he was hardly in a position to start exploring the coast for a more favourable site.

On 21 January, accompanied by a small detachment of marines and a group of officers including John Hunter and David Collins, Phillip rowed north in three boats to explore Port Jackson and Broken Bay. Cook had described them both, but had suggested that they were unsuitable for any sizeable settlement.

On the afternoon of 21 January, Phillip entered Port Jackson. He was later to write that it was 'one of the finest harbours in the world, in which a thousand sail on the line might ride in perfect security'. It was on that first afternoon that Phillip landed on the northern shore of the harbour, encountered about 20 unarmed Aborigines and, thinking them strong and friendly, named the beach they were standing on, 'Manly'. The rowboats then crossed the harbour and near the southern headland established a camp on a beach which, to this day, is called Camp Cove.

Phillip subsequently explored the southern shoreline, eventually finding a cove with excellent deep mooring and a fresh stream which he named Sydney Cove, after Lord Sydney, the British Secretary of State at the time.

All contact with the Aborigines had been friendly. They had been curious about the arrival of strangers and had greeted them more with bemusement than aggression.

On 26 January, Phillip led the fleet, which had been lying at anchor in Botany Bay, north to Sydney Harbour. By the middle of the day, convicts were cutting down trees around the edge of Sydney Cove and, as the day came to an end, Phillip and his officers raised the Union Jack of Queen Anne and toasted the British royal family and the future of the fledgling colony.

Modern Australia began at Sydney Cove. It was there that the country's first convict settlement was established. It was from there that the early explorers departed. And it was from there, spreading out to the north, the west and the south, that the development of the rest of the continent took place.

The settlers and Aborigines

The relationship between the early European settlers and the Aborigines is a history of expediency on the European side and dogged resistance against impossible odds on the part of the Aborigines. It is a sad demonstration of the notion that the conquerors make their own laws. The British expanded into the Australian hinterland with little regard to land ownership and little respect for Aboriginal life.

The observation about Aborigines made by the Reverend William Yate in 1835—'[T]hey were nothing better than dogs, and it was no more harm to shoot them than it would be to shoot a dog when he barked at you'—is a fair summary of the attitudes which prevailed on Australia's numerous frontiers from the end of the 18th century until the middle of the 1930s.

Conflict between Aborigines and Europeans occurred within months of the arrival of the First Fleet in 1788. As early as May 1788 a convict working beyond Sydney Cove killed an Aborigine, and shortly afterwards two convicts were speared and killed while gathering rushes at a place now known as Rushcutters Bay.

Governor Phillip, aware of the potential problems, demanded that a cautious approach be taken. However, when his gamekeeper was speared in 1790 he embarked on an active policy of reprisals. Expeditions were sent out to kill as many Aborigines as possible, and by 1791 Phillip had instituted a policy that any Aborigines attacking whites should be 'made an example of'.

The final major conflict in the Sydney basin occurred in March—April 1816 when Governor Macquarie sent a military expedition to the Nepean, Grose and Hawkesbury rivers with instructions to capture every Aborigine they came in contact with and to shoot all resisters and hang their bodies in the trees. Macquarie's aim was to 'eventually strike Terror amongst the Surviving Tribes'. There is no record of the number of Aborigines killed by the expedition.

This process of indiscriminate killing of Aborigines was to continue with the settlement of Tasmania where, in the

Above: *The trams have gone and the buildings are now lofty skyscrapers, but George Street still winds down to Circular Quay and the Harbour Bridge dominates central Sydney's landscape. This photograph of George Street was taken in 1931.*

space of 72 years, the vast majority of the Aboriginal population was wiped out by a mixture of random killing, government-approved incarceration and active programs of capture.

Within three months of the British colony being established at Risdon Cove in 1804 there was conflict between the military forces and local Aborigines which resulted in a massacre of between 30 and 60 Aborigines. For the next 20 years, atrocities were commonplace. Aboriginal women were tortured and enslaved by sealers. There is evidence that some settlers killed Aborigines and used their bodies to feed their dogs. Symbolic of these atrocities was the story of the Aborigine woman, Truganini, known incorrectly as the last of her tribe. By the time she was 17, Truganini had been raped, had seen her mother stabbed, her uncle shot, her stepmother kidnapped, her sisters captured and kidnapped, and her betrothed murdered.

By the 1820s there was open warfare (sometimes known as the Black War) between the Aborigines and the white settlers. This led to the declaration of martial law in 1828. The final chapter in the history of Aboriginal—European relations in Van Diemen's Land occurred between 1832 and 1876 when successive governments tried to establish settlements for the Aborigines on Gun Carriage Island, Flinders Island and at Oyster Bay. The last of this dwindling group of survivors was Truganini, who died on 8 May 1876. Her bones were finally cremated and her ashes scattered in the D'Entrecasteaux Channel in 1976.

Back on the mainland, the settlement of the country beyond the Blue Mountains led to numerous conflicts with members of the Wiradjuri people whose lands spread to the west of the Great Dividing Range. By the mid-1820s the frontier lands around the present-day site of Bathurst had been turned into a quasi-war zone. It was here that poisoned food was first employed by settlers in an attempt to wipe out the local Aboriginal community.

As the frontier moved further from Sydney, the killing continued. On 26 May 1836 the explorer Sir Thomas Mitchell attacked a corroboree of nearly 200 Aborigines on the banks of the Murray River. On 9 June 1838, on Henry Dangar's Myall Creek station, 12 station hands forcibly removed a group of Aborigines to a nearby stockyard where they shot, stabbed and decapitated them, and then attempted to burn the bodies. This became known as the Myall Creek massacre. The men were subsequently tried and some of them were executed.

As other settlements developed, the same patterns emerged. The Europeans settled the land with no consideration for the indigenous inhabitants, and so conflict became inevitable. In 1834 a small group of settlers to the south of Perth on the Murray River requested military protection against the local Aborigines. A party of police, soldiers and settlers led by the Swan River Colony Governor, Sir James Stirling, was formed specifically to 'punish' the Aborigines, and the ensuing conflict became known as the Battle of Pinjarra.

Europeans moved into the Gippsland area of north-eastern Victoria in the mid-1830s. Records of the massacres which followed are sketchy, but it is now recognised that the person largely responsible for the merciless killings was Angus McMillan, an important local explorer and landowner who subsequently became a member of the Victorian Legislative Assembly and, ironically, the local protector of Aborigines.

Occasionally the Aborigines fought back. At Hornet Bank station in the Dawson River area of central Queensland, members of the local Yeeman tribal group killed nearly all the members of the Fraser family; and, at Cullin-la-Ringo station near Emerald, 19 whites were massacred by a party of Kairi Aborigines.

When Thomas Keneally wrote his novel *The Chant of Jimmy Blacksmith*, he turned a very small chapter in the European—Aboriginal conflict into one of the most famous episodes in Australian history. In 1900, in northern New South Wales, seven whites were killed by Aborigines Jimmy and Joe Governor and Jack Underwood. Subsequently, Joe was shot, and Jimmy Governor and Jack Underwood were

Above: *For nearly a century Truganini was known incorrectly as the last Tasmanian Aborigine to die in captivity. In 1975, descendants of Tasmanian Aborigines scattered her ashes in D'Entrecasteaux Channel near Bruny Island.*

arrested, tried and hanged. The story as told by Keneally is that the killings were the result of racial conflict. Keneally portrays Jimmy Governor as a highly responsible and hard-working man who was constantly taunted by his boss because he had married a white woman.

Skirmishes and killings were to continue well into the 20th century. As recently as 1926, after an Aborigine had killed a European boundary rider near Forrest River Mission in the Kimberley Region of Western Australia, a posse killed an estimated '20 or more' although the local Aborigines put the figure as high as 100. The events of this massacre have been recorded in Randolph Stow's novel *To the Islands*. And in 1928, at Coniston station in the Northern Territory, a policeman named William George Murray formed a posse and rode through the area shooting indiscriminately at Aboriginal camps. The local Aborigines estimated that between 60 and 70 people were shot. When Murray was tried in Darwin he defended his actions, claiming: 'What use is a wounded black feller a hundred miles from civilisation?'

Above: Sovereign Hill is a theme park at Ballarat which recreates the ambience of the Victorian goldfields in the 1850s. Visitors can even pan for gold in the park's stream.

The discovery of gold

From the time Governor Phillip raised the Union Jack on the shores of Sydney Harbour until the discovery of gold in 1848, Australia was essentially a gigantic prison for the detritus of the prisons of the newly industrialised British Isles.

During this 60-year period the British worked assiduously to keep foreigners away from their penal colonies. It is not difficult to work out why they were so paranoid about possible invasions or why they were so concerned about rapid migration of free settlers. Today, there are suburbs on the shores of Botany Bay called La Perouse and Sans Souci. Although few Australians think of these suburbs as being particularly French, they symbolise how close Australia came to being a French colony.

When, on 24 January 1788, Phillip was about to take the First Fleet up the coast from Botany Bay to Sydney Cove, he noticed two French ships riding at anchor off the coast. It must have been a disorientating moment. Phillip had sailed halfway around the world, was about to establish a penal colony on one of the most isolated coasts on earth, and suddenly there were two European ships on the horizon. The ships were commanded by de la Perouse, a French explorer who had left France in 1785 specifically to explore the Pacific.

This French interest in Australia was never converted into an attempt to establish a colony on the continent. This, however, did not stop British paranoia, which was greatly exacerbated by the Napoleonic Wars of the early 19th century. There were numerous attempts—notably at Albany and Perth in Western Australia, at a number of unsuccessful sites near the present-day city of Darwin in the Northern Territory, and around the coast of Tasmania—to develop colonial outposts which would keep the French at bay.

This paranoia managed to keep the colonies 'pure' until the 1840s when the combination of the discovery of gold and increasing pressure to close the penal colonies led to a rapid and dramatic change in the structure and nature of Australian society.

The first discovery of gold had occurred in 1823 when J. McBrien, a government surveyor, found gold in the Fish River near Bathurst. Then in 1839 Peter Strzelecki found gold near Hartley.

'Put it away Mr Clarke or we shall all have our throats cut!', the New South Wales Governor, Sir George Gipps, is supposed to have said in 1844 when a geologist, the Reverend W. B. Clarke, showed him gold which he had found in a creek near Lithgow in New South Wales. Gipps was worried that a public announcement of the discovery of gold, especially in a colony where the majority of the residents were criminals, would cause violence and chaos.

If the government didn't want a gold rush, it was certain that the squatters and farmers didn't. The last thing they wanted was farm labourers leaving their lowly paid jobs to try their luck on the goldfields. So pressure from both the government and rural interests managed to keep knowledge of Australia's gold from the public for 28 years.

However, transportation to New South Wales had ended in 1840, and by the end of the decade the fears of violence that a gold rush might produce had subsided. A mass exodus of the population to California in search of gold caused the New South Wales Government, under Governor Fitzroy, to institute a policy of gold exploration in 1849.

The gold rushes started when Edward Hargraves, after 18 months spent working on the Californian goldfields, returned to Australia with a belief that the area around Bathurst and Orange in New South Wales might contain gold. On 12 February 1851, at the junction of Summer Hill and Lewis Ponds creeks, Hargraves and a colleague, John Lister, successfully panned gold. In April, Lister and two brothers, James and William Tom, found gold at Ophir. In May 1851, Hargraves took 120 grams of gold to Sydney and showed it to the Colonial Secretary, and on 14 May the gold discovery was officially announced. Within days, men were pouring into the Ophir area. The gold rush had started.

The success of the New South Wales goldfields caused a rush of people from Victoria to New South Wales. To stop the exodus, a Gold Discovery Committee was formed and £200 was offered to anyone who could find gold in Victoria.

The Gold Discovery Committee did not have to wait long. Only six weeks after the Ophir announcement, James Esmond found substantial gold deposits near Clunes and within the next eight months the vast deposits at Ballarat and Bendigo had been discovered.

Inevitably the squatters' worst fears became a reality. Farm labourers, indeed anyone touched by gold fever, threw down their tools and headed for the goldfields.

Prior to 1851, Australia's population was concentrated in the major cities (Sydney, with 54 000 people, accounted for 28 per cent of the country's total population) and was increasing in a slow and measured way. Australia had an average of 12 000 free migrants a year from 1832 to 1842. After the discovery of gold the population of the country soared. From 1851 to 1861 it trebled. In Victoria alone it rose from 80 000 to 500 000. In September 1851, 19 000 people landed at Melbourne; in 1852, 95 000 people arrived in Australia.

The majority of immigrants were English, Scottish and Irish. It is true that virtually every nationality on earth could be found on the goldfields, but for the duration of the gold rushes the English, Scottish and Irish were by far the largest

groups. The Chinese, who were later to provoke considerable anger, did not start arriving in substantial numbers until as late as the mid-1850s.

It has been argued that the greatest changes in Australia's history occurred as a result of the 1850s gold rushes. From 1788 to 1851, Australia had been little more than a handful of small colonies, mainly populated by British convicts, police and military personnel, and a small number of squatters and farmers. The white population nearly all came from the British Isles, life was quiet and simple, and the economy of the colonies was dependent on wool.

Then, in a decade, the population of the country exploded. Miners and adventurers arrived from all over the world. The wealth of the colony was measured in gold rather than wool—the Victorian goldfields yielded 22 million ounces. The system of convict colonies was swept away as tens of thousands of free settlers arrived, demanding different rules and regulations, different forms of government; in a few years, the convict element in Australia was unimportant.

With the wealth of the goldfields came a spectacular increase in bushranging. Frank Gardiner and his gang made £14 000 in one hold-up of a coach that was carrying gold. Equally, the sudden population boom created new towns

and seaports and an environment where new roads had to be built, opened up areas which had been unexplored or were only sparsely populated, encouraged the building of networks of railways, and gave a boost to primary and secondary industry.

The result of all this activity was that in the space of 50 years, from 1851 to 1901, Australia went from a collection of British-dominated colonies to independent nationhood.

Anglo-Saxon Australia

One of the issues to emerge from the rapid influx of immigrants during the gold-rush period was the so-called White Australia Policy. The word 'policy' suggests that this was some kind of formal arrangement authorised by Parliament. In fact, it was a series of *ad hoc* discriminatory pieces of legislation designed to keep Australia predominantly English-speaking and Caucasian.

The essence of the 'policy' was the *Immigration Restriction Act* of 1901 which allowed the newly created Commonwealth Government to pick and choose the people it perceived as desirable immigrants. The key to this was a 'dictation test' which could be administered in any European language and which a person applying for Australian citizenship had to pass. Of course, in

Above: In 1886 a gaol was established at Trial Bay in northern New South Wales. Closed in 1903, it is now a museum which records the harsh penal conditions of the late 19th century.

most cases the test was held in English and the vast majority of 'desirable' migrants passed it without any difficulty.

The dictation test remained until 1957. By that time, Australia was recognising that it could not rely solely on English-speaking migrants from the British Isles to maintain its racial purity. In fact, after World War II it became an accepted political orthodoxy that Australia had two options: populate or perish. The Japanese had demonstrated that Australia was vulnerable to attack and invasion. Prime Minister Harold Holt stated the position clearly when he said:

> The danger of invasion by a determined, well-equipped enemy, so clearly disclosed and so narrowly averted, did more than all the political oratory and journalism of the preceding fifty years to convince the great mass of Australians that they must either populate and develop their vast continent or accept the probability of having it taken from them.

After the war the population of Australia was only a little over 7 million. It had been adversely affected by the wartime economy and there was an acute shortage of labour. In 1945, Arthur Calwell was appointed as Australia's first Minister for Immigration. His brief was simple. He had to create programs which would attract European immigrants to Australia.

Calwell developed a policy whereby the natural increase in the Australian population, then 1 per cent, would be matched by a further 1 per cent made up of 70 000 migrants. With this in mind, the government initiated a large-scale drive to attract migrants, and a committee spent six months touring Europe to assess immigrant prospects. It soon became clear, despite Calwell's hopes, that if large-scale immigration was to proceed, most of the immigrants would have to come from countries other than Britain.

Calwell became aware of the plight of displaced persons in International Refugee Organisation (IRO) camps, and of families in Malta and the Netherlands. For the first time, help with passage costs and with finding jobs and accommodation on arrival in Australia became available to non-British migrants. The IRO had 1.5 million displaced persons in its camps at the time. The Department of Immigration applied a rigorous selection procedure to every applicant. Those selected were chosen for their capacity to assimilate into Australian society, and were predominantly young, healthy, male and fair-haired. All successful adult men and single women were required to sign an undertaking to work for two years in any occupation found for them in Australia. The first ship arrived in November 1947 and the migrants were taken to a former army camp at Bonegilla in north-west Victoria.

Over the next five-year period, about 170 000 refugees arrived in Australia. They came predominantly from Eastern European countries such as Romania, Poland, Bulgaria, Russia, Hungary, Czechoslovakia, Yugoslavia, the Ukraine and the Baltic states. Later, a further 10 000 Maltese, 120 000 British and approximately 10 000 others were given assisted passage. Another 160 000 came unassisted, bringing the number close to half a million. The program worked so well that the target was increased to 200 000 a year in 1950.

The displaced persons, in particular, were to challenge many of the accepted tenets of the Australian way of life and herald an awakening of cultural pluralism. Although they were generally better educated than most Australians, all but a few were directed into unskilled work. It wasn't until 1949 that their skills began to be utilised.

The role of these migrants in the postwar reconstruction of Australia cannot be overestimated. With few family ties, no property and little understanding of their civil rights, they were seen as basic labourers and placed in industries that had difficulty attracting Australian-born workers. They formed a major part of the Snowy Mountains Hydro-Electricity Scheme and moved into new industries in the outlying suburbs of Melbourne and Sydney. This immigrant-driven increase in Australia's population continued until the intake was reduced as a result of an economic downturn in 1953.

The brief flurry of immigration had a profound effect on Australian society. The new arrivals may have seemed to be on the edge of Anglo-Saxon Australia, but they gradually became assimilated into the fabric of the society. The racial narrowness which had persisted for nearly 200 years was suddenly torn away and replaced by a very real sense of multiculturalism.

Above: Known for its distinctive architecture and vibrant cafe lifestyle, the historic port town of Fremantle is popular with both tourists and locals.

Australia as part of Asia

Perhaps the most radical reappraisal of Australia's position in the world has been generated by the suggestion that Australia, for all its Anglo-Saxon and European roots, is essentially an Asian country. This argument, passionately presented in recent years by the Australian Labor Party, is a mixture of pragmatism and an acknowledgment that the geopolitical world is changing.

Australia's recognition that it needed to shift its global perspective probably started during World War II when the Prime Minister, John Curtin, decided that Australian troops were needed to protect Australia far more than they were needed to protect British interests in war-torn Europe.

Curtin's argument with Winston Churchill, who still believed that Australia's first obligation was to the 'mother country', resulted in the famous declaration that: 'Without any inhibitions of any kind, I make it quite clear that Australia looks to America, free of any pangs as to our traditional links or kinship with the United Kingdom'.

Curtin acted by repatriating Australian troops from the Middle East to meet the increasing threat from the Japanese. There was no doubt that it was a real threat. On 8 December 1941 the Japanese bombed Pearl Harbour. The war in the Pacific had begun. The first Japanese bombing raids on Darwin, Wyndham and Derby occurred only four months later in March 1942. In the interim the Japanese Imperial Army had blitzkrieged its way through the Pacific, progressively invading Malaya, the Philippines, Hong Kong, Singapore and the Dutch East Indies. The British resistance had been pathetic. The Japanese sank two British warships and grabbed Guam, and their victory in Singapore was described by one Australian newspaper with the following words: 'There have been few more serious miscalculations in all British history'.

The forces the Japanese had unleashed on South-East Asia, and the sheer incompetence and ineffect of the old European colonial forces, were to reap a harvest of independence movements after the war, with regions like

Above: *The Chinese community in Australia dates back to the gold rushes of the mid-19th century. Today, important dates on the Chinese calendar are celebrated by the community with fireworks and traditional dragon dances .*

French Indochina, the Dutch East Indies and British Malaya all seeking independence from their colonial overlords.

It was hardly surprising, given the mood of the time, that Australia also sought its independence. The initial response was one of mixed emotions. Australia both encouraged and feared the new Asian independence movements. Traditionally it had always looked beyond South-East Asia towards Europe. This perception was symbolised by the fact that in 1945 Australia had no diplomatic missions in South-East Asia. Yet, Australia actively supported Indonesia's drive to independence by bringing the conflict before the United Nations Security Council, representing Indonesia on the UN Committee of Good Offices and sponsoring Indonesia's entry into the United Nations forum.

The Japanese had shown Australians how vulnerable they were to outside invasion. It was impossible to police 19 000 kilometres of coastline and, with the emergence of the Cold War, the Korean War and the Communists under Mao Zedong in China, Australia was potentially vulnerable to attack from the

north. This perception was partly based on 'the domino theory', a notion which mixed the belief that communism was eager for world domination with the idea that countries would fall to communism like dominoes and therefore it was only a matter of time before Australia would be invaded. Add to this the belief that Asia was overpopulated and would soon be seeking vacant lands for their crowded millions and it is easy to understand how, between 1945 and 1980, the country's attitude to Asia was driven by fear and a desire to keep the informal 'White Australia Policy' in place.

Whether these fears were rational, they were certainly deeply held. It is hard to define when Australia became more tolerant and pragmatic towards Asia. Certainly the fears were maintained and sustained during the Korean War and the Vietnam War, in both of which Australian troops were actively involved. The orthodoxy in Australia was that if 'they' (meaning Asians in general and the Koreans and Vietnamese in particular) were not stopped 'over there', it was only a matter of time before they would invade the northern coastline.

The changes occurred rapidly. In the 20 years between 1975 and 1995, Australia moved from a country still fearing Vietnam and distrustful of mainland China and Japan to a country which welcomes, and actively encourages, students from all Asian countries. It is a country which abounds in Chinese, Vietnamese and Thai restaurants. A country whose major export destinations define its change of focus. In 1992/93, 24.6 per cent of exports went to Japan, 10.9 per cent to the United States, 5.8 per cent to South Korea, 5.7 per cent to New Zealand, 4.3 per cent to the United Kingdom, 4 per cent to Singapore, 3.3 per cent to Taiwan, 3.2 per cent to Indonesia and 3.1 per cent to Hong Kong.

The idea of Australia as a colonial outpost of Britain is made nonsensical by such figures. When Australian politicians talk about a new focus towards Asia they are talking about a reality, not about some future plan.

Australia today

Modern Australian society is in a state of flux. The changes which have occurred since the 1950s have been dramatic and have far-reaching implications in the way Australians view themselves.

In the 1950s, Australia was still overwhelmingly a monocultural country inhabited predominantly by people of English, Scottish and Irish stock. It was aggressively committed to Britain and had fought beside the British in two world wars. Its trade and economic success was intimately connected to the British economy. Queen Elizabeth II, the British royal family, the British rule of law, and British manners and customs were still seen as a benchmark of sophistication and civilisation. Consequently, the Australian diet was modelled on a British diet. Tea and beer were the dominant drinks. Meat and two vegetables, preferably roasted, were considered a normal main meal. Bread and potatoes were the main sources of carbohydrates. Cold meals consisted of lettuce, tomato, cheddar cheese and cold meats.

If a family ate out, which they did rarely, they were likely to go to a hotel for a main meal which would commonly be roast beef and Yorkshire pudding. They would go to the local Chinese restaurant if they were being daring, and if they were travelling they would stop at a cafe commonly run by Greeks where they'd be served a meal consisting of meat and two vegetables.

Meals are a remarkably good barometer of social change. The elements of Australian cuisine which are now taken for granted would have been deemed alien and strange in the 1950s. The idea of freshly ground coffee and cappuccinos was impossibly foreign. Wine as a preferred drink to beer was inconceivable; and wine bars were places where muscat, sherry and port were served to derelicts and alcoholics. Exotic cheeses, European processed meats such as salami and the rich variety of German wursts, and salad dressings other than mayonnaise, were unknown. Pastas (with the exception of spaghetti, which came in tins) and rice were rarely used.

Perhaps the most defining element of Australia in the 1950s was the fact that the country's success, a success which led the prominent Australian social historian, Donald Horne, to describe it as 'the lucky country', was its vast wealth in primary resources. 'A giant hole in the ground', 'Success on the sheep's back' and 'The mineral bin of the world' were all expressions used to describe Australia's economic base in the 1950s. The country was a major exporter of wool, wheat, beef, mutton, iron ore and coal. It also had huge reserves of bauxite and gold. There was a perception on the continent that secondary and tertiary industries were unimportant when the balance of payments could be controlled successfully by endlessly exporting primary products.

How did Australia change? What is Australia like in the 1990s? It is hard to pinpoint the specific forces which changed Australia. Various writers have argued for elements such as migration, the vision of Prime Minister Gough Whitlam, Patrick White winning the Nobel Prize for Literature, the traumatic sacking of Gough Whitlam by the Governor-General in 1975, the changing circumstances in Europe, the decline of Britain, the economic success of Asia, the maturation of a young society, a growing sense of nationalism and pride, and the need to throw off the shackles of cultural cringe. All have merit, and all are elements of modern Australia.

Modern Australia is a country with a clear yet complex sense of its identity. It is an urban nation (over 80 per cent of the population lives in cities). It is truly multicultural: having successfully

Above: *Australians love sport. Winter sports include rugby league, Australian Rules football and rugby union, including international competitions such as this Sevens match in Sydney.*

THE PEOPLE

Modern Australians

It is easy to assume that Australia is a homogeneous society. On the surface there seems to be a coherence. In fact, there are considerable variations from state to state. These are not variations of language—research has revealed that distinct dialects have not emerged in spite of the relative isolation of Western Australia from the more populous eastern states—nor are there variations in cuisine, clothing, attitudes and values. The greatest variations have been produced by migration. States such as New South Wales and Victoria have absorbed the vast majority of recent non-English-speaking migrants and consequently are much more multicultural than the more rural states. For example, a survey that was carried out in 1994 revealed that 14 per cent of all Australians were born in non-English-speaking countries. Yet, when this was analysed by state, it revealed that only 4 per cent of Tasmanians, as opposed to 17 per cent of Victorians, were born in non-English-speaking countries. This is not surprising. Immigrants have tended to gravitate towards the major cities. There are large non-English-speaking communities in Sydney, Melbourne, Wollongong and Newcastle. Tasmania, which has consistently had an unemployment rate of 10 per cent or worse for the past decade, is unlikely to attract new immigrants because it does not offer work or community support.

Australia is still a sparsely populated country. The population in 1994 was 17.8 million and by the year 2041, it is anticipated that it will have crept up to around 24.8 million. To put these figures into perspective, it is worth remembering that there are 2.3 Australians for every square kilometre and that only French Guiana (1.7), Greenland (0.1), Mauritania (2.0), Mongolia (1.4) and Namibia (1.9) have lower population densities than Australia. It is also worth considering that there are fewer people in the whole of Australia than there are in the greater metropolitan areas of Tokyo, New York and Seoul.

Above: More than 90 per cent of Australians live within 20 kilometres of the coast. Annual surf carnivals, such as this one at Christies Beach south of Adelaide, are a summer tradition.

absorbed the great European migrations of the 1950s and 1960s, it then received a second wave of migration from the Middle East and South-East Asia. Australia rejoices in its diversity.

The cuisine tells the story of modern Australia. It is common for people to have a breakfast of croissants and freshly ground coffee or perhaps muesli. Lunch, which was once a pie or sandwiches, is now a bewildering array of takeaway foods from Asia and Europe, as well as health foods and freshly squeezed juices. A person contemplating a special meal in a restaurant for either lunch or dinner will realistically choose from the cuisines of France, Italy, Greece, China, Japan, India, Thailand, Malaysia, the Lebanon and Vietnam; and, if they want to be truly exotic, they can find menus offering kangaroo, emu and even witchetty grubs.

Australia's wines, ranging from fortified varieties to whites, reds and champagne-styles, often take the honours at international wine shows.

Culturally, the country has been a major force in the international film industry for the past two decades, producing everything from art films such as *The Piano* through to popular entertainment like the *Mad Max* series and light-hearted social comedies such as *Strictly Ballroom* and *Muriel's Wedding*.

Economically the country is still very dependent upon its vast natural resources. However, in recent times there has been a push towards strengthening the secondary and tertiary industrial base. There have been calls for Australia to become 'a clever country', leading the world with innovative inventions and grasping the huge potential of modern electronic technology and the computer-driven world of the information superhighway.

Modern Australia likes to see itself as a tolerant and democratic society. The largest gathering in the country occurs each year at the Sydney Gay & Lesbian Mardi Gras, which attracts up to half a million people and is watched around the country on television. There is a strong movement towards reconciliation with the country's indigenous peoples, and commentators and public figures who espouse racist and bigoted viewpoints are commonly seen as a source of national embarrassment.

Like all societies, Australia has many flaws and many areas which need improvement. Still, as it approaches the 21st century the country is economically strong, is generally compassionate, has a tolerant, predominantly non-violent society, and offers most of its inhabitants a good standard of living with high educational and social expectations.

Above: *A necklace of beaches and rugged cliffs defines Sydney's eastern limit. In contrast, the calm waters of Sydney Harbour are protected from the power of the Pacific Ocean.*

In spite of the inevitable bulge of baby boomers, the median age of Australia's population is 33.5 years. The population is growing at a rate of around 1 per cent a year, with immigration now accounting for only one-fifth of that growth.

Any generalisations about the nature of Australians are difficult. The certainties which defined Australians as predominantly Anglo-Saxon, English-speaking, Christian, socially upwardly mobile, urban-dwelling, egalitarian, sports-loving, and democratic in the 1950s no longer exist. Australian society has become much more complex and multi-layered and consequently most generalisations break down.

Where once Australian towns and cities only had Christian churches—predominantly Church of England, Roman Catholic, Presbyterian and Methodist—now it is common to see Buddhist temples and mosques. In Wollongong, for example, the largest religious building in the city is a huge Buddhist temple; and in Granville, in Sydney's western suburbs, an Iman calls the faithful to prayer from the tower of an elegant, modern mosque. By 1986 Australia had nearly 110 000 practising Muslims, over 80 000 Buddhists, nearly 70 000 practising Jews and 21 500 Hindus. While these figures may seem relatively low, they do reflect changing patterns of migration and an increasing cultural diversity within the community. Of greater significance is the fact that the number of Muslims, Buddhists, Jews and Hindus nearly trebled between 1976 and 1986.

Where once Australian culture was dominated by a sense of Britishness, it is now more multicultural and more aggressively Australian. In the 1950s it was expected that newsreaders on both radio and television would speak with an educated British accent. By the 1970s it had become acceptable to speak with a distinctly Australian accent.

The inevitable cultural domination of the United States has changed the country's language (to a point where most people would now spell 'gaol' as 'jail'); the clothing fashions of popular American sports such as baseball and basketball have become defining fashion statements for teenagers; American movies dominate in the major cinema complexes; and the all-pervasive American fast-food empires—McDonald's, Pizza Hut and KFC—are now integral to Australian society.

Modern Australian suburbia is remarkably similar to American suburbia, with large shopping complexes, huge parking lots, the majority of people driving their own cars, freeways to speed up access, and neat suburban plots where people still build single-storey brick bungalows.

Perhaps the most significant change is that, out of this potpourri of influences, Australia has gradually begun to find its own identity. The sense of 'cultural cringe' which dominated Australia's sense of itself has been largely removed. Australians now want to hear Australian voices on radio and television, they want to take elements of other societies which they find useful and they want to be perceived as Australians rather than as some kind of colonial outpost.

These symbolic changes in the Australian character have occurred progressively since the 1970s. Today the majority of modern Australians want their country to become a republic and see the role of the British monarch as the Australian head of state as irrelevant. They want some kind of genuine reconciliation with the country's indigenous people, and they want Australian Aborigines to be recognised for the uniqueness of their culture and their remarkable tenacity in the face of over 200 years of active discrimination. They want a tolerant society where minority groups are acknowledged and their rights respected. They want a society that is fair and equitable with adequate and comprehensive social legislation to protect those members of society who are incapable of looking after themselves. They are happy to live in a society which enjoys the benefits of cultural diversity. They want their arts—music, literature, drama, painting, and film—to reflect Australian society in all its multicultural complexity.

These are not dimly enunciated platitudes but deeply felt needs by a diverse and complex community which is proud of its peaceful and democratic traditions. Modern Australians are proud of their country and the values it espouses.

A nation of city dwellers

In spite of the active and continuing promotion of rural life as the essence of its society and character, Australia is essentially urban and suburban. Before World War II only one in three Australians lived in cities; today most Australians live in the urban strip which stretches around the coast from South Australia through the states of Victoria and New South Wales to Queensland. There is an additional small concentration of population along the coastal strip of the south-western parts of Western Australia.

Over 70 per cent of Australians live in Darwin, Canberra, the state capitals and the six cities which have populations in excess of 100 000. To put this into clearer perspective, Sydney is home to 62.8 per cent of the population of New South Wales, Melbourne has 70.3 per cent of Victoria's population, Brisbane has 44.8 per cent of Queensland's population (this uncharacteristically low figure is the result of Queensland having a number of major coastal city ports, notably Cairns, Townsville, Mackay, Bundaberg, the Gold Coast and the city of Whitsunday), Adelaide and Perth have 73 per cent of their respective states'

populations, Hobart has 40.2 per cent of Tasmania's population and Darwin has 46.6 per cent of the Northern Territory's population. The low figures for Hobart and Darwin are a result of the size and importance of Launceston in Tasmania and Alice Springs in the Northern Territory.

In total, more than 85 per cent of Australians live in urban areas. While there has been a reaction against this intense urbanisation (the country's rural population actually increased from 13.9 per cent to 14.5 per cent between 1976 and 1986), the inevitable fact is that such population concentrations tend to produce a snowball effect and continue to attract more and more people. Thus, new immigrants prefer to live in Sydney and Melbourne. It is hardly surprising that companies wishing to expand their operations will choose a major city where there is a skilled work force, sophisticated transport infrastructure and large markets. This has meant that the state capitals have continued to grow, while other centres have been unable to offer serious competition. In the case of New South Wales and Victoria, the cities of Sydney and

Melbourne are so dominant that they account for nearly 40 per cent of the country's total population and the two states are home to more than 60 per cent of the country's population.

One variation on this urbanisation theme has been the expansion of large coastal centres since World War II. These centres have become commuter belts for the major cities. In Queensland the Gold Coast, once little more than a collection of sleepy seaside holiday villages, has become the state's second-largest population centre. Similarly, in New South Wales the development from Gosford to The Entrance, which has been accompanied by the building of a freeway and the establishment of a fast electric commuter rail service, has been spectacular. Similar developments have occurred along the Mornington Peninsula near Melbourne, along the western shores of Gulf St. Vincent near Adelaide, and to the north and south of Perth. These commuter zones have not established their own individuality. Rather, they have tended to mimic the prevailing urban home styles. This has produced a lack of architectural variety and differentiation. In spite of the vast distances, it is therefore common, for example, to find the same standard three-bedroom, brick veneer project home in both the commuter belt north of Sydney and the urban area south of Perth. This has led to a suburban uniformity across the country.

The Australian character

Australia is a young country. It only came into existence with the federation of the states in 1901. Before that it was a collection of competitive states which were so incapable of agreement that they all had different rail gauges and they sent separate military forces off to fight Britain's wars.

With federation there was an instantaneous rush of pride and nationalism. This newly discovered nationalism led to a search for the essence of the Australian character. That search, which started as early as 1910, began with a notion of mythical heroism and gradually evolved into an understanding of the nature of 'the average Australian'.

Above: *Although over 80 per cent of Australia's population lives in towns and cities, Australians see themselves essentially as rural dwellers. These stockmen at Hamilton Downs station are still symbols of the 'real' Australia.*

The country was less than ten years old when a reader of the hugely popular *Lone Hand* magazine suggested that Australians abroad were not liked because they were 'provincial, unreliable and had an irrepressible tendency to blow, brag and skite'. It was like an attack on a favourite son. As a result, the correspondence pages lit up with deeply felt anger. The writer J. H. M. Abbot summed up Australian pride when, replying to this perceived slur on Australian nationhood, he asked:

And in cricket and football have Australians proved their unreliability against England's best teams? Did Lord Kitchener suppose them to be 'unreliable' in the war, when he had every troop of them in the fighting line, whilst 90 000 British regulars, militia and South African volunteers defended the lines of communication? It almost seems that the Australian has a pretty fair right to an 'irrepressible tendency towards bragging'.

It was an interesting and illuminating attempt to define character. Australians were good at sport, and ferocious and brave in battle. This perception did not appear from nowhere. Since the 1880s, when nationalism began to emerge and *The Bulletin* gave voice to a generation of poets and prose writers, there had been a fascination with the Australian character. When the writer Joseph Furphy described his novel *Such is Life* to the editor of *The Bulletin*, he declared: 'I have just finished writing a full-sized novel: title, Such is Life; scene, Riverina and northern Vic; temper, democratic; bias, offensively Australian'.

Furphy, along with the bush poets Andrew 'Banjo' Paterson and Henry Lawson, had defined the Australian character in rural terms. They saw the true Australian as brave, hard-working, fiercely independent, distrustful of authority, a loner, laconic of wit, and free from the destructive impulses of class, racism and jingoism which had so defined Europe.

When Paterson wrote the poem 'Waltzing Matilda', he was reaching deep into the Australian psyche; his solitary 'swagman' (an itinerant hobo) would rather commit suicide than be arrested for stealing a sheep from a landowner.

Similarly, when Paterson wrote 'The Man from Snowy River', he sang the praise of independence, of raw bush courage, and of a humble, unassuming battler who was strong and brave but unwilling to draw attention to himself.

This notion of Australians was clearly articulated by Joseph Furphy in *Such is Life* when he wrote:

Without doubt, it is easier to acquire gentlemanly deportment than axe-man's muscle; easier to criticise an opera than to identify a beast seen casually twelve months before; easier to dress becomingly than to make a bee-line, straight as the sighting of a theodolite, across strange country in foggy weather; easier to recognise the various costly vintages than to live contentedly on the smell of an oily rag.

The message was simple: urban values were not to be trusted; the skills of a bushman were to be admired. This rather romantic notion was given extraordinary potency by World War I and the battles Australians fought near Gallipoli in Turkey. Coming less than two decades after the formal creation of the country, they became defining moments for the national character.

C. E. W. Bean, Australia's official war historian, wrote of the Australian soldiers in *The Official History of Australia in the War of 1914—1918*:

It lay in the mettle of the men themselves. To be the sort of man who would give way when his mates were trusting to his firmness; to be the sort of man who would fail when the line, the whole force, and the allied cause required his endurance; to have made it necessary for another unit to do his own unit's work; to live the rest of his life haunted by the knowledge that he had set his hand to a soldier's task and had lacked the grit to carry it through—that was the prospect which these men could not face. Life was very dear, but life was not worth living unless they could be true to their idea of Australian manhood. Standing upon that alone, when help failed and hope faded, when the end loomed clear

Above: *Aboriginal painting is the most ancient art on earth and in recent years their dot paintings have become both fashionable and expensive.*

in front of them, when the whole world seemed to crumble and the heaven to fall in, they faced its ruin undismayed.

It was statements like this, combined with the assertions of rugged individualism by the bush poets, that created an image of the Australian character which was to persist until the 1970s. Over the next 50 years, various people—particularly sportspeople and actors—would come to symbolise 'the true Australian'. The first was Snowy Baker, a truly remarkable sportsman (he played 26 sports and was New South Wales open swimming champion at age 13 and, at age 18, won the Australian middle and heavyweight boxing championships on one night) who, after the war, became a successful actor and the archetypal 'bronzed Aussie he-man'.

As Australian society began to change, so too did the blind assertion that the 'true Australian' was a rugged, sporting bushman. The realisation that Australia was an urban society and that the typical Australian was more likely to sit behind a desk or work in a bank made the sun-tanned image seem naive, romantic and inaccurate.

The most significant challenge came from Donald Horne, a social historian, who wrote *The Lucky Country*. Horne's astute observations about modern Australian society called into question the old assumptions.

Horne was followed by a number of perceptive observers who concluded that while egalitarian impulses, a laconic sense of humour and a general easy-going nature were aspects of the Australian character, it was also true that few Australians had an understanding of rural life and that urban living had little to do with being a fine sportsman and a resilient loner.

This is an ongoing debate. Australians have had less than a century to define themselves. Having developed few truly Australian cultural artefacts and having borrowed from other societies and cultures means that, at any time, it is almost impossible to articulate those things that are most typically and enduringly Australian.

Australia's indigenous people

It is one of the great, and often ignored, truths of Aboriginal life that the strength and vitality of their indigenous culture lies partly in their ability to adapt to changing conditions and circumstances.

If, as some anthropologists have assumed, it took nearly 10 000 years for Aborigines to disperse through the Australian continent and to reach the extremities of Tasmania and Western Australia, then surely it is reasonable to assume that the lifestyle of each small group would develop subtle but nevertheless significant variations.

Although Aboriginal language and tribal groups can be large—for example, the Wiradjuri people of New South Wales lived in an area covering tens of thousands of hectares—the family or clan groupings are usually small.

The last Aborigines to live truly tribal lives unaffected by European culture were the Aborigines of the Western Desert of Central Australia. They were absorbed into missions and out-stations as recently as the 1950s. Their daily lives were recorded on film and revealed a lifestyle carefully considered and modified to fit their environment. The small autonomous groups comprised no more than 8—15 people. Each person had his or her own particular job, with the women being responsible for looking after the youngest children, collecting berries and seeds, and grinding the seeds into flour to make a kind of damper bread. The men were responsible for catching small animals such as bandicoots, lizards and birds. Because food was scarce they would persist in the hunt of an animal. In some cases they would dig up to 2 metres into the ground after a bandicoot if they had seen it disappear down a hole. The men used their spears and spear throwers to catch larger animals such as kangaroos and wallabies. Such catches were not to be expected. The desert environment was unforgiving and a kangaroo was regarded as a rare feast.

The group had a carefully considered cycle of hunting and gathering which was based on using, but not over-using, a number of waterholes. It was as though the cycle was used to allow the land to

Above: *The finest displays of Aboriginal rock art, readily accessible to the traveller, exist in Kakadu National Park.*

regenerate. The group would stay near one waterhole for perhaps a week or a month, depending on the fertility of the local area and the availability of food. When it was considered that the area should be allowed to regenerate, the group would move to another, already well-known, waterhole. In some instances, this would involve a walk of up to 100 kilometres.

For tens of thousands of years, Aborigines lived this kind of hunter—gatherer lifestyle. It was a common misconception of Europeans that the Aborigines were Stone Age people held forever in some kind of historical aspic. This was simply not the case. They understood fully the complex cycles of existence in Australia—particularly the devastating effects of El Niño—and had adjusted their lifestyle accordingly.

The quality of Aboriginal life has been another issue debated by anthropologists. Were they living harsh, unpleasant lives before the Europeans arrived, or were they living a near-perfect life in harmony with their environment?

In *Conquest of the Ngarrindjeri*, Graham Jenkins writes about the Aborigines who lived along the southern coast of South Australia:

Above: *The Aboriginal flag has become a symbol of pride and cultural identity for Australia's indigenous population.*

The most outstanding example of the Ngarrindjeri's genius lies in their ability to live so richly and so harmoniously with each other and with their land. They were a truly classless society and had reached the apogee as far as refined egalitarian socialism is concerned. Yet if they had to be placed in any European class scale, their mode of life could only be compared with that of the old aristocracy. Their dedication to cultural pursuits—the ballet, music, opera and art; their enjoyment of pomp and ceremony; their strong adherence to ancient codes of chivalry and etiquette; the pleasure they derived from sports and hunting; their great personal courage, pride and independence; their insistence on the right of an initiated man to bear arms and for honour to be honourably defended; their epicurean approach to food; their honest acceptance of human passions and lack of hypocrisy regarding them; these and other aspects of Ngarrindjeri life find distinct parallels in the outlook and way of life of the European aristocracy. The great difference lay in the fact that in Ngarrindjeri society everyone was an aristocrat. The Ngarrindjeri showed this world that it was possible for socialism and the aristocratic lifestyle to be married harmoniously, and for life to be a rich cultural and creative experience – without servants and without masters.

If Jenkins is right, then what Europeans did to Aboriginal society is almost beyond description. Over 200 years, the white settlers of Australia systematically tried to destroy Aboriginal culture. They raped the women and killed the men. They forced the people off the land which was so integral to their livelihood and belief systems. They desecrated their sacred sites and, unaware of Aboriginal diversity, placed different groups together in mission stations and reserves. They separated children from their parents. By the best estimates, the population of Aboriginal Australians more than halved in less than 100 years.

From 1788 until the 1980s, white Australians had little respect for Aboriginal religion or belief systems. The obsessive fascination with the 'primitiveness' of Aborigines and the belief that all 'savages' could be saved from eternal damnation by conversion to Christianity were such powerful paradigms that for two centuries Europeans simply could not imagine that the Aborigines might have complex and subtle belief systems of their own.

In recent times, white Australians have begun to recognise the importance of Aboriginal beliefs (even if, in some instances, they still have trouble grasping the concepts) and that Aborigines have a special, and sacred, relationship with the land. This has impacted dramatically on Aboriginal land claims.

Further acceptance of Aboriginal spirituality and religion occurred with the discovery of a cremated Aboriginal woman near Lake Mungo in western New South Wales in 1970. The combination of cremation and the unusual discovery that the bones had been broken into small pieces and placed in a pit suggested some kind of religious rite. The fact that carbon dating suggested the age of the bones to be some 38 000 years old meant that this was clearly the first example of human cremation and there was the possibility that a society which cremated and prepared bones had a belief system. Could it be the Aborigines had the oldest religion on earth?

There is a tendency to underestimate the importance of religion in Aboriginal life. This misconception is based on the Western paradigm of physical and visible signs of religion—churches, images of deities and so on. In 1986, two anthropologists, Rhys Jones and Barbara Meehan, reported that during an extended stay with the Anbarra people they had noted that rituals took up to 40 work-hours a day, while catching food took less than two hours.

Similarly, the corroboree, a source of fascination for Europeans but often misinterpreted as just a primitive dance, was eventually understood for the important and complex ritual it is.

In *Aboriginal Mythology*, Mudrooroo defines a corroboree as 'a Koori word, perhaps from the Eora language, which has been taken into English. Roughly, it means a dance or ceremony. The suffix, "boree" shows that it refers to the boro circles, or ceremonial grounds'.

On one level the corroboree was a vital part of Aboriginal social life. The lack of substantial food supplies in Australia meant that small Aboriginal groups rarely made contact with their larger language community. This only occurred when suitably large food supplies—bogong moths in southern New South Wales, bunya pine nuts in southern Queensland—were available to feed the 500–1000 people who gathered.

These corroborees were vital to the fabric of Aboriginal life. With most Aborigines living in small groups of 15–30, it was imperative that marriage occurred outside the immediate group to prevent inbreeding. Corroborees kept the tribal gene pool dynamic.

The most remarkable feature of Aboriginal society is that, for all the misunderstanding and open antagonism displayed by the Europeans, it survived. While modern Aborigines are often still treated as second-class citizens and many live in substandard conditions, there has been an observable improvement. This has been the result of a combination of legislation and an increasing perception that Aborigines have not been treated fairly and that the problems of the past need to be rectified.

On a purely political level, the 1960s and 1970s were a major watershed. On 3 March 1949, legislation had been introduced into the country's Federal Parliament to allow Aborigines to vote in federal elections. Up to this time, no Aborigine had enjoyed any political rights. This was the beginning of a change in official attitudes towards Aborigines which culminated in the 1967 referendum which, for the first time, gave the Commonwealth Government the power to legislate for Aboriginal people and gave Aboriginal people the right to vote. It is a comment on the mood of the time, and the level of awareness of the Australian people, that 90.8 per cent of them voted in favour of the changes.

It was followed in the 1970s and the 1980s by the granting of land rights to the Gurindji people at Wave Hill, the declared intention that in future there would be 'self-determination for indigenous Australians' and the subsequent handing over of Uluru (known to white Australians as Ayers Rock) to the custody of the local Aborigines.

Modern white Australian society has made genuine attempts to resolve the long-running conflict between Europeans and Aborigines. Symbolic of this process was the law passed on 22 December 1993 in the Federal Parliament which acknowledged that the concept of 'terra nullius' was nonsense. It was a genuine attempt at reconciliation, recognising that Australia was inhabited before the Europeans arrived and that, within 200 years, the indigenous culture had been altered and nearly destroyed.

In 1788 there were over 300 000 Aborigines in Australia. Some 200 years later there were nearly 18 million Australians, of whom only 265 000 were Aborigines. European society impacted savagely on Aboriginal society. The Aboriginal population of Australia in 1921 was estimated to be only 72 000.

Above: *There is nothing quite like Uluru anywhere else on earth. To watch it, particularly at dawn or dusk when it is changing colour, leaves one struck with wonder at its beauty.*

Australia: a multicultural society

Although there was a commonly held perception up until the 1950s that Australia was essentially an emigrant Anglo-Saxon society, this was never entirely accurate. Since the First Fleet, the country has had ethnic and racial minorities. The country's first bushranger was an escaped convict, John Caesar (known as 'Black' Caesar), a native of Madagascar. Little is known of Caesar's early life. There is no record of how he got from Madagascar to England, but the most likely explanation is that he was a seafarer working on ships plying the East Indies route. In early 1785, Caesar was caught picking pockets around the London docks. He was gaoled and on 14 May 1785, was sentenced to seven years' transportation. He arrived at Sydney Cove with the First Fleet. It is also known that amongst the First Fleeters there was another man of African descent who was known as 'Black Jemmey'. In total during the entire penal colony era, some 900 convicts, of whom 120 were born in Britain, were non-white.

While 900 non-white convicts hardly constitutes a richly diverse social and racial mix, there was also the issue of Irish Catholics and English Protestants. There has been a tendency to gloss over the differences, but the fact that Governor Phillip, when he took his oaths of loyalty on 13 February 1788, formally declared that he did not believe the bread and wine actually became the body and blood of Christ during the Lord's Supper, was a clear statement of the early colony's anti-papist stance.

Given that a number of the convicts on the First Fleet were Irish and many were, at least nominally, Roman Catholic, Phillip's declaration must have been divisive. It is a sad commentary on the religious inflexibility of the early settlers that the first recorded Roman Catholic mass on Australian soil did not occur until May 1803 and that the first officially appointed priests did not arrive in the colony until 1820.

The first substantial shipment of Irish convicts (133 male and 22 female) arrived on 26 September 1791 aboard the *Queen* from Cork. By 1820 a total of

6891 Irish convicts had arrived in Australia. These numbers continued to increase dramatically and by 1853, when transportation to Australia ended, a total of 29 466 males and 9104 females, nearly one-quarter of all convicts sent to Australia, were of Irish descent. It is significant, although hardly surprising, that over 90 per cent were Roman Catholics.

While the presence of black convicts and Irish Catholics indicates that the early settlers were not exclusively white Anglo-Saxon Protestants, the truth is that the overwhelming majority were and that they would determine the attitudes and values of Australia for the next century and a half.

However, Australia was an extremely vast, largely unsettled land and it could not maintain any kind of British Protestant racial purity. For example, nearly 500 labourers from the Indian subcontinent were brought to Australia between 1837 and 1844. Between 1838 and 1839, a group of some 500 Lutherans from Klemzig in Prussian Silesia arrived in South Australia. They settled outside Adelaide in settlements they named Klemzig and Hahndorf and, in the next decade, established the vineyards which would become the backbone of the Australian wine industry. A few of the famous personalities involved in the early days of the wine industry included J. E. Seppelt, T. G. Hermann Buring and Benno Seppelt.

Other small groups—the famous Afghan camel drivers who provided one of the vital forms of transport in the desert areas of central Australia, and the diverse groups who arrived on the goldfields in the latter half of the 19th century—came to the country and subsequently settled there. Still, by the end of World War II, Australia was an aggressively Anglo-Saxon society looking towards 'mother England', determined to maintain strong links with the British monarchy and believing strongly that the British legacy—in terms of the country's legal and political systems—was part of a great heritage which should never be altered.

It is one of the miracles of modern Australia that these deeply entrenched

Above: *This Lutheran church, located at Tanunda in the heart of South Australia's fertile wine-growing area, epitomises the significant impact German immigrants had on the area.*

notions have, in the space of 40 years, been questioned, challenged and, in many instances, altered.

Jewish settlers

The Jews represented a very minor racial grouping amongst the first convicts. No one knows the precise number, but there were between eight and 14 Jewish convicts on the First Fleet when it sailed into Sydney Harbour in 1788. Like the Irish Catholics, the Jews were not allowed to practise their religion. The main difference between the two groups was in their size and political commitment. While it is true that every convict ship to arrive in Australia had some Jews aboard, by 1830 only 400 Jewish convicts had arrived and by 1845 there were only 800.

Perhaps the most fascinating aspect of this small immigration was that a Jew named John Harris became Australia's first policeman and one of the convicts, Isaac (Ikey) Solomon, was a famous London fence and was said to be the model upon whom Charles Dickens based Fagin in *Oliver Twist*.

The first Jewish religious services were held in George Street, Sydney, in 1828. They were organised by Philip Joseph Cohen who had been given authority to preside over marriages by the Chief Rabbi in London. In 1830, Aaron Levy became Australia's first Jewish rabbi and the following year permission was given for the Jews in the Sydney community to practise their religion. The first synagogue was opened in 1844.

In 1851 there were still only 2000 Jews in Australia. A decade later, largely due to the gold rushes which had brought people from all over the world, the Jewish population had increased to 5000. Few of the Jewish immigrants worked as miners. They were absorbed into the life on the goldfields as pedlars and gold purchasers. Still, they constituted a sufficiently large group in the goldfield communities for synagogues to be built in both Bendigo and Ballarat.

As the goldfields became less profitable, the number of Jewish immigrants declined. This changed dramatically in the 1880s when a wave of anti-Semitism spread across Eastern Europe, sending many Jews fleeing from Russia and Poland to the United States, Britain and Australia. In spite of a further emigration from Eastern Europe after World War I, the Jewish population of Australia declined in the inter-war years. More than 30 per cent of Jewish men were marrying outside the faith, and by 1933 only 0.36 per cent of the country's population was Jewish.

The rise of Nazism in Germany caused a dramatic turnabout. By 1938, 2000 Jews from Germany, Austria and Czechoslovakia were seeking refugee status in Australia every week. By the time war was declared the following year, only 8000 Jews had managed to emigrate to Australia.

Inevitably, the end of World War II, and the end of the Holocaust, resulted in a renewed desire to emigrate. By 1966 the Australian Jewish community was three times the size it had been in 1933. This inevitably meant that Jews became more involved in Australian public life. Today they are an integral and a significant part of the country's cultural and political life.

Chinese on the goldfields

By far the most significant non-white emigration to Australia started between 1848 and 1852 when 3000 Chinese, most of whom worked in near-slavery conditions, arrived to work as indentured labourers on farms.

Their arrival saw the first clear signs of racial disharmony in the country's non-Aboriginal population. The 'coolies', as they were derogatively termed, were paid as little as £1 a month (about a quarter of the wage paid to the equivalent white workers) and this was widely interpreted as a threat to the stability of the white work force.

The situation was greatly exacerbated by the massive immigration which occurred during the 1850s. The discovery of gold, combined with the end of convict transportation, did much to change the nature of Australian society. In Victoria in 1854 there were only 2000 Chinese. Over the next 18 months, 15 000 Chinese arrived on the Victorian goldfields and by 1858 there were an estimated 40 000 Chinese in the state.

By 1861, 60 per cent of all the people on the New South Wales goldfields and 25 per cent of those on the Victorian goldfields were Chinese. In total, Chinese workers accounted for 7.5 per cent and 6.5 per cent, respectively, of the male populations of Victoria and New South Wales.

This massive influx of Chinese workers challenged the essentially European nature of Australian society. With their long pigtails the Chinese looked different. They worked in groups, lived in separate communities, spoke a different language, had different religious beliefs, ate different food, and showed no desire to settle in Australia or to integrate with the predominantly Anglo-Saxon local community. Yet, the nature of the legal system and the essential fairness of the goldfields ensured that for most of the time they were protected by local laws.

However, racism did emerge. Tolerance was easy when there was plenty of gold for everyone. It became a very different issue when gold became sparse and the Chinese, because they worked in groups, started reworking old diggings. Miners began to see the Chinese as locusts swarming all over the diggings. There were protests on the Victorian fields, with miners heatedly demanding that the government introduce legislation to slow down the rate of Chinese migration.

In 1857, at Buckland River, close to 2500 Chinese were forced off the goldfield by an angry mob of European miners. A large number were injured and there is evidence that three subsequently died from exposure.

At Lambing Flat in New South Wales, in 1861, 2000—3000 gold miners attacked the Chinese camps. It has been estimated that over 400 Chinese were injured and a number died in the riot. It is a comment on the racist nature of the attack that the *Sydney Morning Herald* described the Chinese camp at Lambing Flat in these terms: '[A] neater little canvas town could not be found. The Chinese here were making fair wages; they were industriously plying their callings and interfering with no-one.'

The law may have protected the Chinese, but public opinion ensured that they were quickly relegated to the status of second-class citizens. By 1855, Victoria had enacted legislation which ensured that every Chinese person entering the colony had to pay £10. There was also a limit on the number of Chinese arriving on ships. These laws were difficult to enforce, and it became common for Chinese goldminers to arrive in South Australia (particularly along the Coorong, which was near the Victorian border) and to travel overland—usually on foot—to the Victorian goldfields.

The Victorian legislation was followed by restrictive legislation in South Australia (1857) and New South Wales (1861). These pieces of legislation had been repealed by the end of the decade.

Perhaps the most remarkable facet of Chinese immigration in the 1850s was that once goldmining, and particularly alluvial goldmining, came to an end, most of the miners chose to return to China. Those who remained did not congregate in communities, but rather dispersed themselves throughout rural Australia. The census of 1871 revealed 54 towns and 75 rural districts with Chinese populations of up to 10 people.

A second wave of Chinese immigration occurred in the 1880s when gold was discovered in the Northern Territory and northern Queensland. Once again, the Chinese became the predominant group on the goldfields.

The antagonism towards the Chinese was openly racist. There was a perception that Australia was a European outpost on the edge of Asia and that any moment it would be overrun by Asian hordes. It was always an issue of 'There are so many of them and so few of us'. Finally, there was also a generally held perception that the Chinese had little interest in Australia beyond the extraction of its gold.

Above: *The Chinese were actively discriminated against on the Australian goldfields.*

From this narrow view it was a short step to the *Northern Miner*'s infamous editorial which argued that 'Kanakas and Chinese are distinct types of the genus Homo—some would go so far as to deny that they belong to the human family at all'.

It was out of such bigotry that Australia developed what would eventually become known as the White Australia Policy. Before 1901, various states had enacted legislation which clearly discriminated against the arrival of non-Anglo Saxons. In Queensland there was an unrelenting campaign to stop Asian immigration.

This became a reality in 1876 when a tax of £9 6s 8d was charged for every ton of rice that was imported and the mining fees of the Chinese were increased from 10 shillings to £3. The Chinese protested that the government had broken the fundamental tenet of British democracy, 'No taxation without representation', and even the British Government refused to ratify what they saw as openly discriminatory legislation.

The real precursors of the White Australia Policy were the *Aliens Act* of 1876, which meant that no naturalised Chinese could submit themselves as candidates for either Queensland House or Parliament, and the *Chinese Immigrants Regulation Act* of 1877, which insisted that £10 be paid by every Chinese entering the colony of Queensland and that Chinese immigrants be restricted to one person for every 10 tons of a ship's capacity. This latter piece of legislation proved so successful that in 1883 the impost was raised to £20 and in 1888 the number of immigrants was restricted to one person for every 500 tons of a ship's capacity.

It seemed that once the legislative ball started rolling, there was no way to stop it. In 1886, legislation was introduced to prevent Chinese holding homestead leases and mortgages, and by 1891 no Asiatic or African could lease any land in a mining district. This was pushed even further when one C. S. Mein, in the Queensland Legislative Council, argued that, 'The right to mine the goldfields of this colony was an inherent right of British subjects—inherent in those who

Above: *The exquisite Chinese Gardens near Darling Harbour in Sydney have been designed on gardening principles that date back to the 5th century. Within the gardens are miniature mountains, lakes, waterfalls, forests and flowers.*

had succeeded through the power and the expenditure of money and force of the British Empire', which led to the Chinese being restricted to fossicking.

By 1898 the legislation had become so discriminatory that the Chinese were effectively banned from goldmining. The Queensland legislation meant they could not work on a new goldfield until Europeans had worked it for three years, they could not own or lease land near a mining site and, although they could still obtain a miner's licence, it could only be used for fossicking.

Under such circumstances it is hardly surprising that one of the first pieces of legislation enacted by the new Australian government was the *Immigration Act* of 1901 which made it

difficult for anyone who was not of Caucasian stock to enter Australia. This policy was to continue, not so much as clearly stated government policy but rather as an implicit racist assumption, until the 1980s. In the early years it was prosecuted without subtlety. Pacific Islanders who had been brought to Australia to work on the canefields were forcibly repatriated to their islands, and Chinese were actively discriminated against. This continued until the end of World War II and was still in place, but being used with more subtlety, until the 1970s when the reality of living on the edge of Asia and the realisation that Asians could make significant contributions to the life of Australia began to lead to changes in policy.

Kanakas in the canefields

One of the most unfortunate chapters in Australia's multicultural history occurred between 1863 and 1904 when 61 160 Pacific Islanders arrived to work on the Queensland canefields. The problem was that many of the people who arrived—they were known as 'Kanakas'—were indentured labourers who worked in a state of virtual slavery. To give some idea of the true nature of the treatment of Kanakas there is a photograph, taken in the late 1800s and now held in the archives of CSR (the Colonial Sugar Refining company), which depicts a half-naked Pacific Island woman tied to the mast of a sailing ship much to the amusement of a large group of sailors. The situation depicted is no different from that which existed in the American Deep South before the Civil War. Not surprisingly, the photograph has never been published.

The first Kanakas arrived from the New Hebrides and Loyalty Islands aboard the 100-ton schooner, *Don Juan*, on 15 August 1863. The ship carried 67 indentured servants who were to be employed by Robert Towns on his 4000-acre cotton plantation on the Logan River. There is little doubt that Towns and his fellow plantation owners were seeking cheap labour and that their intentions were driven only by the thought of profit. They tried to rationalise their position, claiming 'to make the immigration of Melanesians a temporary aid to us and not to encourage their permanent settlement in the country', but those people who saw beyond their motives realised that the importation of 'black labour' was a recipe for racial division, the creation of a racial underclass, and the introduction of a kind of slavery into Queensland at a time when the United States was involved in a civil war to end slavery.

In 1884 the Queensland politician William Brookes articulated the fears of humanitarians when he told the Legislative Assembly: 'The evil of coloured labour was that it placed the servile labourer too much under the control of the white man. They might not call it slavery, but it was akin to it—cousin to it.'

In fact, Brookes was being polite. In many instances it was unambiguous slavery. The term applied to the process was 'blackbirding'. It had started as early as 1847 when Benjamin Boyd brought South Pacific Islanders to New South Wales to work on his sheep stations when he experienced a shortage of labour due to the gold rushes.

From the beginning the process had slavery written all over it. On 26 April 1867, Ross Lewin, who was to become one of Australia's most successful blackbirders, advertised that he could provide the 'best and most serviceable natives to be had in the islands at £7 a head'. In theory, what he was offering for £7 was an indentured labourer. Statistically, the islanders who came to Australia were overwhelmingly male and aged between 16 and 30. Only 6 per cent of the islanders were women.

It has been estimated that approximately one-quarter of the island labourers were kidnapped by 'recruiters' who enticed them by barter or forcible abduction. The usual term of 'indenture' was three years. It is accurate to say that while the Kanakas were not slaves, they had few freedoms during that three-year period and they arrived in Queensland with little concept of the work or the nature of the conditions they were agreeing to.

The employment of Kanakas was a result of a series of complex economic forces. With the advent of the American Civil War, the cotton mills in England had been eager for Australia to create a cotton industry. The actual picking of cotton balls was a tedious, unpleasant, back-breaking activity. In America it had been done by slaves. Experiments in Australia with Aborigines, a group of 1200 Indian labourers and Chinese workers from the goldfields had all failed. There had even been a request for the reintroduction of convict labour to sustain the infant cotton industry. In a way, the Pacific Islanders were a last resort by an industry desperate for cheap and efficient labour.

There was further pressure on the labour force from the continuing discovery of gold. Graziers working in isolated areas of Queensland were having great trouble attracting labour and it was felt that the importation of indentured labour would go some way to solving this problem. In fact, any chance of the Kanakas solving this rural labour shortage was eliminated in 1877 when the *Polynesian Labourers Act Amendment Act* insisted that no Pacific Islander could be employed more than 30 miles from the Queensland coast.

This restrictive legislation was extended in 1884 when the *Pacific Island Labourers Act* was amended so that Kanakas could only work in the sugar industry. This legislation, some of the most racist ever enacted in Australia, allowed Kanakas to do only the most menial tasks connected with the sugar industry. They were not allowed to work in the refining process, and the women were not allowed to be employed as domestic servants. They were not allowed to become British citizens and did not enjoy any of the basic rights afforded to Australian residents.

Although maltreated, the Kanakas were vital to the development of the Queensland sugar industry. It was a sad truth that sugar prices around the world were, without exception, the result of the use of cheap labour. If Queensland had not had cheap labour, it would not have been able to compete with sugar from the islands of the Caribbean.

Above: *For decades South Pacific Islanders were virtual slaves on the huge sugarcane fields of northern Queensland.*

The constant complaints about maltreatment of the South Pacific Islanders, and regular scandals about blackbirding in the South Pacific, meant that by the 1890s there was a serious attempt to get the Queensland sugar industry on a sound economic footing without the use of cheap island labour. The problem was partially solved by the arrival of Italian immigrants who were prepared to work on the sugar plantations.

The increasing antagonism towards non-Caucasians, caused largely by action against the Chinese on the goldfields, resulted in legislation being introduced into the Queensland Parliament to restrict the rights of both the Chinese and the Pacific Islanders. This was the legislation which evolved into the White Australia Policy. When the *Immigration Act* was passed by the new Federal Government in 1901 it authorised the deportation of any Kanakas found in Australia after 1906. The only exceptions were those people who had lived in Australia for 20 years or more, had married in Australia or who owned property. The period of the Kanakas came to an end when 3600 people were returned to their islands at the end of 1906. Any analysis of this sorry period

is inevitably influenced by considerations of the forces which were at work. There is no doubt that the actions of people like the blackbirder Ross Lewin border on slavery. After he was caught shipping 100 Banks Islanders to Fiji in 1869, Lewin was charged with slavery but never convicted.

There is little doubt that the vast majority of Kanakas came to Australia with little idea of the work they were expected to do. But it is clear that the owners of sugar and cotton plantations saw the Kanakas as a form of cheap labour. However, it is true that, regardless of the morality involved, the Kanakas did help to establish the sugar industry in Queensland which endures and, for the past 90 years, has successfully operated without cheap labour.

European immigration

After World War II, Australia began an active campaign to attract migrants of European descent. Preference was given to British migrants, who were offered assisted passages from 1947 until 1972 when the program was expanded. As a result, by the mid-1970s Australia had immigration assistance plans in place with Italy,

Greece, Holland, West Germany, Yugoslavia, Poland and Austria.

The postwar immigration boom had brought 1 million migrants to Australia by 1955. The first wave brought refugees from war-torn Europe, mainly from Eastern European nations. The second wave of migrants, in the 1950s and early 1960s, came from Mediterranean countries, with Italians making up a third of the intake (equal to the number of British migrants). In that period, around 70 000 refugees arrived, including 14 000 Hungarians fleeing the political unrest which followed the 1956 uprising in that country. These migrants formed a new working class and provided essential labour for new manufacturing ventures such as the motor vehicle industry. The 1960s were a period of great prosperity, and most Australian manufacturers could not have functioned without migrant labour.

Until the late 1960s, immigration policy was based on the need to populate the continent and provide workers for Australian industry. On the whole it was successful and, while discrimination existed against Asian migrants, this was slowly broken down. Restrictions on immigration were reduced in 1966 but over the next 10 years the numbers allowed in were also cut. In the 1970s the policy was dominated by family reunions. Access to Australia worked on a points system without racial discrimination. While this continued to be a priority, in the next decade Australia established a refugee resettlement program and a Special Humanitarian Program, a scheme to resettle people whose civil rights were constantly violated in their home countries. Most of the migrants who settled under these schemes were Asian-born but, despite support from both the Liberal and Labor parties, public debate over the number of Asian migrants and refugees Australia can successfully assimilate continues. It is an issue which provokes strong feelings among Australians. Politicians eager to win easy votes will often raise the spectre of too many migrants in an attempt to appeal to the racist elements which still exist in certain communities within the country.

Above: *The postwar immigration program, which actively campaigned to attract migrants of European descent to the country, changed the Anglo-Saxon face of Australia forever. These happy immigrants arrived from Europe on the* Empire Brent *in 1948.*

Above: *The Mediterranean immigrants who arrived in Australia in the 1950s tended to settle in inner-city areas. The Italians, in particular, helped to define the Australian lifestyle. Lygon Street in Melbourne is a true 'Little Italy' with a wide variety of excellent restaurants.*

Arrival of the Italians

The postwar years saw a huge influx of migrants from Italy and Greece. More than any other minority groups, the Italians and Greeks have both had a profound effect on the Australian way of life. It is hard to imagine an Australian city without pizzas, pastas, wines and cappuccinos. Games like soccer have become an integral part of Australian culture, while Australian Roman Catholicism has been changed dramatically from the dour Irish variety to a more buoyant Italian version.

Italian immigration to Australia is essentially a postwar phenomenon. There was one convict of Italian descent on the First Fleet. By the time of the first census in 1871 this had only increased to 960 Italians—a surprisingly low figure given the importance of Italian activists on the goldfields during the 1850s. Raffaello Carboni, who wrote *The Eureka Stockade*—the most important primary account of Australia's only major civil insurrection—was a significant figure during that brief uprising.

A substantial number of Italians came to Australia in the 1890s to work on the Queensland canefields. The cemetery near Innisfail has a distinctive section of imposing Italian family mausoleums.

Like most European countries, Italy was unstable and very near to ruin during the years between World War I and World War II. This economic turmoil led to large-scale emigration. The 1921 census revealed that there were over 8000 Italians in Australia. By 1933 this figure had grown to 26 500. Already the Italians had become Australia's largest immigrant group after the British and the Irish. This inevitably produced racial tensions. In Queensland, local workers protested that their jobs on the canefields were being endangered by Italian workers; and at Kalgoorlie in Western Australia an anti-Italian riot occurred after an Italian bartender got into a fight with a local footballer. Around this time, the Italian fruit-pickers in the Leeton—Griffith area of New South Wales were also subjected to racial vilification.

This anti-Italian feeling persisted. Italians were branded 'dirty dago pests', Fascists or members of the Mafia. This antagonism continued throughout World War II when 3500 Italians were arrested and imprisoned on the assumption that they were supporters of Mussolini.

In spite of all this potential discord, an agreement was reached between Australia and Italy after World War II whereby the Australian Government agreed to provide assisted passage to selected Italian families. In the period 1945—73, about 20 per cent of the Italian immigrants to Australia came on this program of assisted passage.

The issue of race persisted but it was becoming clear that with Australia's fear of possible Asian invasion and its need to increase its population quickly, it was not going to attract enough people of British descent. Consequently, between 1945 and 1973, 379 000 Italians emigrated to Australia. The main reason for the emigration was that Italy had been devastated by the war. The German and Allied forces had engaged in numerous battles in Italy from mid-1943, and many of the cities and large areas of the countryside had been left in ruins.

The vast majority of Italians arriving in Australia found work as labourers. Most of the important postwar industrial development of Australia involved Italian workers. They were prominent in the construction of the Snowy Mountains Hydro-Electricity Scheme, they worked in the booming building industry, and they were employed in the iron and steel and car manufacturing industries.

Italians saw Australia as a land of opportunity and, in substantial numbers, they escaped from labouring and established their own businesses. By the 1980s, more than 20 per cent of first-generation Italians were self-employed, operating small corner stores, working as greengrocers, running cafes and restaurants, and managing their own construction companies.

The importance of the influence of Italian immigrants on the Australian lifestyle can never be overstated. Above all other groups they have helped to define the new Australia. Their wines, coffees, foods and outdoor restaurants, as well as their enduring commitment to a culture which promotes and celebrates outdoor living, have all had a profound impact on modern Australia. There are some social historians who argue that the ambience of modern Australia is closer to Italy than to Britain.

Arrival of the Greeks

The Greeks are the fourth-largest ethnic group in Australia. After the British, Irish and Italians, Greeks form a significant minority with over half a million Australians claiming Greek ancestry.

Few Greeks came to Australia at the time of the gold rushes. In fact, as late as 1891 there were fewer than 500 Greeks living in Australia and by 1939 this number had only risen to 15 000. The major period of Greek immigration started with the government's program of assisted passage in the early 1950s. Between 1953 and 1956, over 30 000 Greeks arrived in Australia. This pattern of migration continued into the 1960s, with an average of nearly 16 000 Greeks a year arriving to settle in the country. The 1970s saw a slight reversal in the migration trend, with many of those who had come to Australia in the 1950s returning to Greece to spend their retirement in the village of their birth.

Although the Greeks are now well established as an important community in the country, their impact on the Australian way of life has been less apparent. Greek restaurants are part of the country's multicultural life, but Greek cuisine has made little impact on Australian eating habits. Feta cheese and retsina wine are all still specialist items, and Greek coffee is still only available in areas where large numbers of Greeks reside. In spite of this, it has long been argued that Melbourne has the second-largest Greek population in the world, with more Greeks than any other metropolitan area after Athens. This may not be strictly correct as there are very large numbers of Greeks living in New York, and the second-largest city in Greece, Thessaloniki, currently has a population of nearly 400 000.

While the impact of the Greeks on Australia has been more subtle than that of the Italians, they certainly have established themselves as successful small business people owning cafes, restaurants, fruit and vegetable shops, service stations and other businesses. Many of them have become active in politics—particularly in Labor Party politics. Prominent political Greeks include Senator George Georges, Andrew

Above: *In recent years there have been significant numbers of South-East Asians, including Vietnamese and Malaysians, who have settled in Australia.*

Theophanous and Senator Nick Bolkus. Greeks have embraced the Australian way of life with enthusiasm and have successfully integrated into Australian society within a generation.

Arrival of the Lebanese

By 1991 there were 75 400 Lebanese living in Australia. They had been arriving since the 1950s but, with the beginning of an extended period of civil unrest and religious conflict in Lebanon in the 1970s, the trickle soon became a flood with many people applying for entry under refugee status.

The first Lebanese arrived in Australia in the 1880s. In most cases they were Christians fleeing Turkish religious oppression; these early immigrants were few in number. By 1901 there were 1700 people of Syrian-Lebanese birth living in Australia and by 1933 this figure had only increased to 3200.

The period of major emigration of Lebanese to Australia occurred in the 1960s. It was the result of a combination of forces. The modernisation of the Lebanese rural economy after World War II resulted in improved farming methods and led to many land-holding farmers moving to the cities. Small num-

bers of these rural dwellers, once uprooted, kept moving and sought residency in Australia. When this was combined with the country's political unrest the trickle of emigrants became a small flood. In 1965, 2000 Lebanese emigrated and 1970 saw more than 24 000 new arrivals.

Although the Lebanese who sought refugee status in Australia were predominantly Christian, there were a significant number of Muslims. This was an important development for Australian society which, up to this time, had been almost exclusively Christian. The arrival of Muslims, and the subsequent construction of mosques in the major cities and the wearing of the black veil, presented Australia's overwhelmingly Christian community with people whose customs and beliefs many found alien. The Lebanese were also important as the first significant group of emigrants from the Arab-speaking world.

The smallness of the emigration, combined with the tendency of the Lebanese Muslims to settle near mosques and their desire to stay within their own communities, meant they went largely unnoticed. However, there was also a significant number of people of Lebanese background who were eager to be absorbed into the Australian community. They often changed their names, and many became successful and well-known business people.

Asianisation of Australia

Geographically, Australia is an anomaly. Located on the Pacific rim, its neighbours are, with the notable exceptions of New Zealand and the Pacific Islands, all Asian. Australia resisted settlement by Asians and actively discouraged Asian immigration for a century after the 19th-century gold rushes.

The changes occurred very slowly. In the 1950s the Colombo Plan brought students from the countries of Southeast Asia—notably Singapore, Malaysia, Pakistan, India and later Vietnam, Thailand and Cambodia—to Australia to study. Their numbers were expanded as Australia permitted fee-paying students from Asia to study at secondary and tertiary educational institutions.

In 1956, Asians who had lived in Australia for more than 15 years could become naturalised Australians. Two years later the 1901 *Immigration Restriction Act* was abolished, and by the 1970s there was a steady trickle of Japanese and South-East Asians.

The current position is that Asians are welcome in Australia and they are coming to settle in increasing numbers. The number of Australians of South-East Asian origin in 1991 was 404 600, an increase of 156 per cent on the 246 900 who were resident in 1981. The increase of immigrants from northeast Asia was even greater, with the numbers increasing 244 per cent from a low base of 56 800 in 1981 to 195 600 in 1991. The largest Asian groups in Australia in 1991 were the Vietnamese (133 400), Malaysians (84 100), Filipinos (74 300), people from Hong Kong (73 200), China (68 500) and India (65 400). They hardly constitute the threat which had so worried politicians in the 19th century and they have made a significant contribution to the diversity and cultural richness of the society.

Commitment to multiculturalism

Today, Australia is a genuinely multicultural society. The forces which have evolved over the past two centuries have slowly coalesced to produce a society which, while English-speaking and still committed to many British legal and political structures, is a diverse mixture of races, cultures, religions and customs.

Whether Australia is a successful multicultural society is still an open question. It is almost impossible to measure such blurry, ill-defined concepts. Is Australian society racist? Inevitably, there are sections of the community that are. There is a small, but active, right-wing section of the community which believes that the country is being overrun by Asians, that the glories and virtues of the 'British way of life' are disappearing, and that there are too many non-Christian, non-English-speaking people in positions of power and authority.

Australia has still not reached a position like the United States where first-generation immigrants such as Henry Kissinger, Irving Berlin, Albert Einstein and Arnold Schwarzenegger have become an integral part of the country's social fabric. While Australian political life, for example, is still dominated by Anglo-Saxons, it is significant that the Federal Ministry formed in May 1993 included such non-Anglo-Saxon names as Andrew Theophanous, Nick Bolkus, Chris Schacht, Con Sciacca, Janice Crosio and Michael Lavarch and had a Prime Minister, Paul Keating, who was inordinately proud of his Irish ancestry.

THE CHALLENGE OF CONSERVATION

Modern Australia is a nation which has been built on the exploitation of its natural resources. There is an unkind joke about the development of Australia which argues that the country's success has been based on: 'If it moves, shoot it; if it's growing, cut it down; if it's in the ground, dig it up.'

The dilemma facing Australia is how the country can balance its economic need to continue exploiting its natural resources with an equal need to preserve the environment. This pressing issue has become known as 'ecologically sustainable development'.

This development covers the range of environmental problems Australia will face over the next 20 years. Water quality, particularly in the inland river systems during periods of drought, is a major problem. The problems associated with the preservation of the Great Barrier Reef, Australia's most spectacular natural tourist attraction, are immense. And the need to develop sound policies on greenhouse emissions, feral animals, pollution and endangered species is a constant challenge.

In spite of all its good intentions, Australia is still confronted with major environmental problems. It is rich in uranium, which is widely seen as a lucrative but dangerous mineral. It has had a timber industry for 200 years, but the insatiable demands of the world are outstripping its ability to regenerate forests and consequently there is constant pressure to log old-growth forest areas. It is a modern society designed around the truck and motor car and consequently its levels of gas emission and

Above: *Green Island, off the coast of Cairns, is one of the most popular outer reef islands on the Great Barrier Reef. It boasts a resort and also attracts numerous daytrippers.*

general road pollution are far too high. The importance of grazing agriculture has resulted in wide-scale clearing of land and the extinction of numerous native species.

One of the greatest dilemmas facing the Australian environmental movement has been the problem of how to deal with native forests which have been seen, for most of the nation's European history, as resources to be cut down and sold to the highest bidder. It is a sad reflection on the approach of Europeans to Australia's vast forests that during the past 200 years half of all the continent's forest areas have been cut down and an alarming 75 per cent of the rainforests have been destroyed.

Prior to 1788, over 15 per cent of Australia was covered with forest and woodlands, ranging from the tropical rainforests of north Queensland through the great eucalypt forests of the Great Dividing Range to the dramatic forests of jarra and karri in the south-eastern areas of Western Australia. Today, only 5 per cent of the country is covered with true native forests and only 0.3 per cent is covered by true rainforest.

Woodchipping

In 1990, the then Director of the Australian Conservation Foundation, Phillip Toyne, spelt out the problems posed by woodchipping when he wrote: 'Our forest ecosystem is being degraded, small saw-mills are closing, Australian tax payers are subsidising the massive profit of Japanese woodchipping and 90 per cent of our best forests are being fed into the chipper.'

The problem was simple. Australian native forests were being used as woodchips in an attempt to meet an ever-growing world demand for paper. The original intention had been to make use of residual wood left on the forest floor, but the demand for woodchips was such that an active program of felling native forests started. The consequences have been profound. Not only have small logging operations been forced out of business, but highly mechanised woodchip mills now dominate the economies of old timber towns without offering the local communities many new jobs.

Above: *The extensive karri gum forests of the south-western parts of Western Australia are dramatic and shady.*

The real problem has been the fundamental inequity of the woodchip industry. Over 70 per cent of Australia's timber exports are in the form of woodchips. From this the country earns around $350 million, which environmentalists like the Australian Conservation Foundation argue does not even cover the costs of maintenance to roads, forestry research and the problems of fire fighting and weed control in cleared areas. Each year, $2 billion worth of paper and timber products are imported. The dilemma is obvious. Exports of $350 million and imports of $2 billion produce a gross financial inequity.

Destruction of the rainforests

Before 1788, 1 per cent of Australia was covered by rainforest. In 200 years that small area has been reduced by 75 per cent so that there are now only 20 000 square kilometres of rainforest left in Australia.

The reason for concern about the rainforests lies in the incredible faunal and floral diversity and the delicacy of the ecology. For example, the wet tropical forests of north Queensland cover a mere 0.1 per cent of the country but contain 25 percent of all plant genera.

In recent times there have been few serious attempts to preserve Australia's rainforests. State governments, with little concern for ecology, have built roads which have produced serious soil erosion and pollution, and opened parts of the rainforest to rapid and destructive secondary growth. Add to this the environmental problems involved in building hydro-electricity power stations and dams in Tasmania, the construction of access routes for tourists, and the continued logging of sensitive regions in Queensland, New South Wales, Victoria and Tasmania, and the need to protect Australia's rainforests becomes obvious and urgent.

The need to protect

One of the major conservation battles in Australia has been the continuing attempt to protect old-growth forests. In essence, old-growth areas contain large old trees which are both standing and fallen. The importance of these areas is that the hollows in old trees are used by many of Australia's endangered species. Whereas the timber industry looks upon old-growth forest as an ideal source of timber and argues that the clearing of old growth results in regenerated regrowth areas, the environmentalists see the trees as being important homes for animals like the sooty owl, the eastern pygmy possum, forest bats and yellow-bellied gliders, and argue that it can take as long as 200 years for eucalypts to develop the hollows which are vital for the existence of these species.

They also argue that old-growth forest, because of its stable forest floor and well-established root systems, is critical for river catchment areas and helps to provide clean water for the local rivers. A forest recently logged will produce soil runoff which is likely to pollute rivers.

Mining and the environment

No industry has experienced such a turnaround in public perception as the Australian mining industry. In the 1950s and 1960s the mining industry was seen as the centrepiece of Australia's buoyant economy and the industry most responsible for the country's high standard of living. Companies like BHP, the country's largest iron and steel manufacturer, were admired for their mineral exploration and exploitation. Companies like Comalco and CRA had huge mineral interests stretching from Western Australia to the north Queensland coast, and their production of iron ore in the Hamersley Range in Western Australia and bauxite at Weipa on the coast of the Gulf of Carpentaria was seen as part of the economic success of Australia.

Mining industry figures still indicate its importance to the economy. It accounts for nearly half of all Australia's exports. In 1989/90 the mining industry accounted for $21.8 billion, with black coal being worth $5.8 billion, gold $2.9 billion, alumina $2.7 billion and iron ore $2.1 billion. Of the world's known deposits, Australia had nearly 60 per cent of the reserves of zircon, nearly 40 per cent of bauxite reserves, and nearly 20 per cent of lead reserves.

Increasing environmental awareness has cast doubt on techniques used by mining companies. They have been criticised for their lack of concern for the environment, their inability to regenerate mined areas, their whole approach to conservation and their lack of respect for the environment.

The litany of ecological crimes committed by mining companies on the Australian environment stretches from one end of the country to the other. The most famous, or infamous, and the most visible, is Queenstown in Tasmania which is a symbol of how mining, with no thought for the environment, can destroy an area. Its hills have been stripped of timber to fire the copper smelters. Furthermore, for decades the hills remained denuded as a result of the sulphurous fumes from the smelters which prevented new growth. The local river was appallingly polluted, and the town nestled in a valley which had the appearance of a deserted moonscape.

Equally serious has been the pollution of ground water by the uranium mine at Roxby Downs in South Australia. Radiation leaking into the water table endangers all life in the area.

While the mining industry cannot be described as a good environmental citizen, it has made serious attempts to

Above: Cape Tribulation is an area of unspoiled beauty where heavy rains and tropical heat produce a hothouse for the rich vegetation that is characteristic of the rainforest.

improve its public image. The issue of sandmining, and its likely effects on the environment, was a major battleground during the 1970s. Today the mining industry claims that its attempts to restore areas where sandmining has occurred have been successful.

While its work is not perfect, the environmental lobby acknowledges that Australia is now a world leader in the rehabilitation of degraded land. Environmental battles in Australia will continue. For example, the burning issue

of uranium mining in the Kakadu National Park and Arnhem Land is still unresolved. A long-running battle to save areas of wilderness in Tasmania from loggers, from governments eager to build roads and from the state's hydro-electricity commission is likely to stretch into the next century. A commitment to maintain the rare beauty of Australia will prove vital not only for our present survival but so that future generations can also marvel at the uniqueness of this most ancient of continents.

NEW SOUTH WALES

Opposite: *The busy heart of Sydney and its surrounding suburbs.*
Above: *A detail on the moulded facade of the restored Queen Victoria Building.*

New South Wales, with its breathtaking capital city of Sydney, site of the first European settlement in Australia, can justifiably lay claim to being 'The Premier State'. Not only is New South Wales the most populated state, but Sydney—with its world-famous Opera House and imposing Harbour Bridge—is the chosen destination for most tourists arriving in Australia from overseas, as it is the logical starting point for any exploration of the country.

A large percentage of the population resides in the narrow strip of land sandwiched between the dramatic coastline and the Great Dividing Range which runs the entire length of the state. Most people live in one of the three major cities of Sydney, Newcastle (in the beautiful Hunter Valley), or Wollongong, or in the many substantial seaside townships which stretch from the Victorian to the Queensland border.

The Great Dividing Range, the most prominent natural feature in the region, is a series of low mountains rising from the coastal plain. At various points—notably in the Blue Mountains to the west of Sydney and the Snowy Mountains near the Victorian border—the peaks are spectacular, soaring majestically above the surrounding landscape. Characterised by a number of box canyons with sheer cliffs and broad flat valleys, the Blue Mountains derive their evocative name from the misty-blue illusion created by the eucalypts that grow on the slopes. The more rugged and dramatic Snowy Mountains attract thousands of eager skiers during winter.

Beyond the Great Divide much of western New South Wales is flat sheep country. With low rainfall, the area is dependent on the Murray—Darling river system for its water supply. Although the state's land use is dominated by agriculture, only 7 per cent is under crops. Sheep and cattle farming predominate. In comparison, nearly half of the coastal plain is utilised for purposes other than farming. The huge steel towns of Newcastle and Wollongong and the urban sprawl of Sydney are typical of coastal land use, with tourist towns such as Port Macquarie, Coffs Harbour and Byron Bay spread out along the coast.

Previous pages: The view from Mrs Macquarie's Chair across to the Sydney Opera House, with the Harbour Bridge and North Sydney in the background, is one of the city's most inspiring sights.

Left: Darling Harbour is a mixture of restaurants, gift and curio shops and conference facilities surrounded by hotels. It offers free entertainment on weekends and is close to the Maritime and Powerhouse museums and Sydney Aquarium.

Below: Since 1788 Sydney Cove, now Circular Quay, has been Sydney's emotional centre. Today it is the city's ferry terminus and is edged by the Opera House and The Rocks.

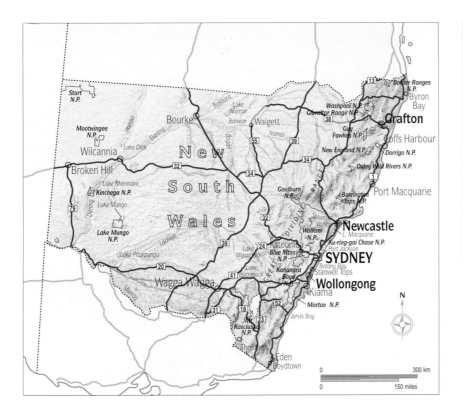

Top: *The Overseas Passenger Terminal, situated on the west side of Sydney Cove, was the disembarkation point for thousands of European migrants arriving in Australia during the 1950s and 1960s.*

Above: *Since its completion in 1932, the Sydney Harbour Bridge has been both a vital link between the northern and southern sides of the harbour and the city's most famous symbol.*

Left: *In recent times the sandstone warehouses at The Rocks have been beautifully restored and converted into gift and curio shops, and fine restaurants, where patrons can enjoy superb views across Sydney Cove to the Opera House.*

Left: On Boxing Day, yachts from all over the world leave Sydney Harbour to race down the eastern coast of Australia, across Bass Strait and down the coast of Tasmania to Hobart. The start of the annual Sydney—Hobart Race is spectacular to watch, especially when the boats sweep through the Sydney headlands.

Below: The Sydney Heads are craggy protectors against the mighty fury of the Pacific Ocean. Here, a ferry from Circular Quay to Manly crosses the narrow opening to the ocean to reach the protection of North Head. In the foreground is Middle Head. When the seas are too rough, the service is cancelled and travellers are forced to make the journey from the city to Manly by road.

Left: Held on Australia Day, the ferry race in Sydney Harbour is an annual event that attracts thousands of onlookers to the harbour's foreshores, and a colourful flotilla of large and small boats. The race is a celebration of the vital part played by ferries in the city's transportation network.

Below left: *Although Sydney's many surf lifesaving clubs were originally created to patrol beaches, they hold regular competitions to display and thereby improve their surfing skills.*
Below right: *Modern Bondi is an exciting mix of top restaurants, fast beach food, surfers, sunworshippers, and even skateboarders and cyclists who display their prowess on the beach's promenades and specially constructed ramps.*

Left: *Sydney's most famous beach, Bondi, is well known because of its proximity to the city centre and because it has always attracted a rich cross-section of the city's multicultural population as well as foreign tourists. In recent times, it has become a prime location for major celebrations by young travellers on New Year's Eve.*

Above: *To the north and south of Bondi, the cliffs rise dramatically out of the Pacific Ocean. Cliff-top homes and apartments vie for spectacular ocean views in this beautiful part of Sydney. It is believed that Bondi got its name from the Aboriginal word 'boondi', meaning the 'sound of waves breaking on the beach'.*

Left: Located near Katoomba in the Blue Mountains, west of Sydney, is the much-photographed outcrop known as the 'Three Sisters'. Frequently climbed, the peak is the most visible symbol of the beauty of this area. Visitors to Echo Point can gaze beyond the Three Sisters across the wild and rugged Jamieson Valley.

Below: One of Katoomba's most spectacular attractions is the Skyway, a modern cableway which runs across one of the box canyons near the town. This is definitely not for the faint-hearted, as passengers can see the valley below between the boards on the floor of the carriage.

67

Above: The New South Wales south coast is cattle and timber country. Watered by rivers like the Bega, the soils are rich and, even during periods of drought, the grasslands provide excellent fodder.

Right: On the far south coast of New South Wales is Boydtown, a deserted whaling station named after its founder, Ben Boyd. The town's most prominent building, which is still standing, is the Ben Boyd Tower—a reminder of a time when the whaling industry sustained the local economy.

Opposite: Considered by many to be the finest coastal view in New South Wales, the outlook from Stanwell Tops south towards Wollongong is quite spectacular. This is one of the few places on the Australian east coast where the mountains seem to tumble into the Pacific Ocean. The Australian aviation inventor, Laurence Hargrave, carried out early experiments here.

Left: *In winter, the Snowy Mountains are covered with snow, transforming the area into the country's premier ski destination. In summer, the mountain air is cool and bracing, and pretty alpine flowers abound.*

Below: *The summer months are an ideal time to explore the Snowy Mountains. Australia's highest peak, Mount Kosciusko (seen here in the background), is a pleasant day's walk from any of the resorts.*

Right, top: *In winter icy Arctic winds sweep across the southern parts of Australia bringing snow to these mountains.*

Snowy Mountains

Right, bottom: The chairlift at Thredbo transports skiers to the top of ski runs where they can enjoy some of the best skiing available in the Snowy Mountains during winter. During the fine days of summer, it takes walkers to the beginning of a hiking trail which leads to the top of Mount Kosciusko.

Following pages: In far western New South Wales, Lake Mungo, once part of a great inland network of lakes, lies on the edge of the central Australian desert. In the 1970s, skeletons of Aborigines dating back 35 000 years were found in the inhospitable terrain. Lake Mungo is now recognised as a significant Australian prehistory site.

Broken
Hill

Top: *Rising out of the desert near Broken Hill is a series of interesting stone sculptures which form part of the Broken Hill Sculpture Park.*

Above: *For most of the 19th century, Australia's agricultural wealth was based on its rich wheat fields and vast herds of sheep. Today, fat lambs and wool are still an important part of the country's rural wealth.*

Right: *Port Macquarie lies north of Sydney on the New South Wales coast. Like so many coastal towns its pretty beaches are a magnet to tourists seeking a leisurely seaside holiday of surfing and fishing.*

Left: *Although a series of low-lying mountains, the Great Dividing Range is often cut by sheer cliffs such as these, where the Apsley Gorge Falls tumble over the escarpment to a pool and fast-flowing river below.*

Above: *A popular holiday destination on the north coast of New South Wales, Coffs Harbour is known for the 'Big Banana', a huge model of a banana beside the highway which has been developed into a theme park.*

AUSTRALIAN CAPITAL TERRITORY

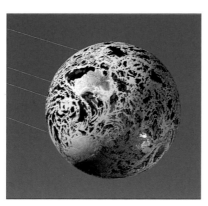

Opposite: Hot-air balloons drifting over Lake Burley Griffin in Canberra.
Above: An outdoor sculpture at Canberra's National Gallery.

Given that the Australian Capital Territory (ACT) came about as a result of intense rivalry between the governments of New South Wales and Victoria, its unique location and beauty come as something of a surprise. When the *Commonwealth Constitution Act* of 1900 was passed, and the Commonwealth of Australia was formally created, the states agreed that a Commonwealth territory should be established to accommodate the new Australian Federal Government. The bitterness that existed at the time between New South Wales and Victoria ran so deep that the Constitution actually stated in section 125 that the Commonwealth territory should be no less than 100 miles (160 kilometres) from Sydney and that it should not be less than 100 square miles (260 square kilometres) in area.

Many sites were investigated and, in 1908, a large area (2330 square kilometres) of sheep grazing country, stretching from the plains of the Southern Highlands through to the foothills of the Snowy Mountains, was chosen. The Commonwealth of Australia formally took possession of the land on 1 January 1911.

During discussions about a suitable site, King O'Malley, a larger-than-life politician, declared that it was necessary to 'have a cold climate chosen for the capital of this Commonwealth. I want to have a climate where men can hope. We cannot have hope in hot countries'. In reality, the capital, Canberra, suffers climatic extremes: in winter, the temperature regularly drops below freezing as winds off the Snowy Mountains whip through the valleys, while in summer, dry heat in the district can sap the liveliest of spirits.

Canberra's strong sense of civic pride and its beautiful location more than make up for this, however. Low-lying hills rise around the city and from the graceful foreshores of Lake Burley Griffin the reflections of elegant government buildings and open parklands are exceptional. Outside the city, the mountains offer quiet roads and bushwalks and, beyond, vistas of rich grazing lands that are transformed by the winter rains to a luxuriant green in spring.

Above: In 1988 a superb new Parliament House was built on Canberra's Capital Hill and was designed so that people could walk to the top of the building and admire the view. It houses both the House of Representatives and the Senate.

Right: In spring, Canberra's parks and gardens are transformed by spectacular floral displays. Visitors flock to the annual Floriade Flower Festival in Commonwealth Park.

Above: Designed by the American architect and town planner, Walter Burley Griffin, the administrative capital of Australia is a city of broad boulevards and elegant circuits.

Left: Canberra is a geometrically precise city with a street grid made up of circles and axes. One of its central axes runs from Parliament House, across Lake Burley Griffin and up Anzac Parade to the War Memorial—an impressive old building commemorating those Australians who fought and died for their country in major conflicts from the Boer War through to Vietnam.

QUEENSLAND

Opposite: Deep inlets and sheltered bays are features of the Whitsunday Islands.
Above: Huge tree ferns are a distinctive part of Queensland's rainforests.

Queensland boasts the warmest, most perfect weather in Australia. The Great Barrier Reef, golden beaches and warm waters attract visitors from all over the world. Yet, for all its warmth and tropical charm, Queensland is rich in contradictions. The northern coastline is often battered by cyclones and drenching rain during the summer months.

Covering a total area of 1 727 200 square kilometres, Queensland is the second largest state in Australia. Within its boundaries there is great physical diversity—the south western corner is desert, while parts of Cape York and north Queensland are impenetrable rainforest and swampy, mangrove wetlands. It is hardly surprising that most of the state's 3 million people cling to the coast, residing in the state capital of Brisbane, the extended cities of Whitsunday and the Gold Coast, the holiday area of the Sunshine Coast, and other major cities such as Townsville, Bundaberg, Cairns and Rockhampton.

The Tropic of Capricorn, 650 kilometres north of Brisbane, divides the state equally between the tropical and subtropical zones. Similarly, the Great Dividing Range forms a natural division between the coastal plain and the vast Artesian Basin of western Queensland.

A narrow strip of rich, fertile soil, essential to the state's sugarcane and dairy industries, runs the length of the coast from the Gold Coast in the south to Cairns and the Daintree Forest in the north. Beyond the coast, the Great Dividing Range rises steeply, its narrow gorges and sheer cliffs notable for their dense rainforest and numerous waterfalls. On the other side of the Range, the marginal plains of western Queensland are vital to the state's sheep and cattle industry.

The Great Barrier Reef, one of the finest natural wonders of the world, stretches from Cape York to Bundaberg—a veritable daisy chain of coral reefs and islands. Evoking all the romantic splendour of the tropics, many of these islands, such as the Whitsundays, are famous for their luxurious resorts; others, equally verdant, are uninhabited. The Reef remains one of Australia's premier tourist attractions, with activities ranging from scuba diving to fishing.

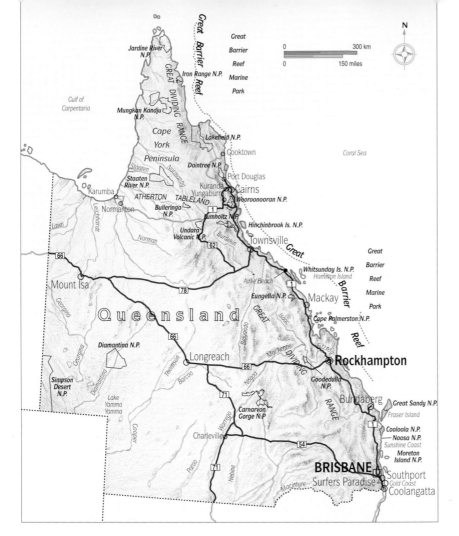

Opposite top: *Queensland's hot, humid climate has resulted in a unique style of architectural home called a 'Queenslander' by the locals. It is characterised by wide verandahs and an open area underneath to allow the prevailing breezes to cool the entire building.*

Opposite bottom: *A popular retreat from the sizzling summer heat is the artificial beach and swimming area at the old Expo site on the southern bank of the Brisbane River, only minutes away from the bustling city centre.*

Left: *The Brisbane River lies at the heart of the city, edged by parks and gardens. The river was once an integral part of Brisbane's transportation network. Today, the ferries travel between the city and the numerous islands which lie to the east of it.*

Above: *The graceful arc of the Brisbane River forms a natural barrier for the city's vibrant and bustling central business district which, like most modern cities, rises in a series of skyscrapers.*

Opposite right: *The construction of Brisbane's Parliament House, an impressive and gracious building situated on the hill above the Botanical Gardens, began in 1865 and was completed in 1889. Solid colonnades, which keep the interior cool during the long, hot summers, are an imposing yet practical feature of the building's design. The architect, Charles Tiffin, was awarded the commission to build Parliament House after winning a national competition with his fine interpretation of the French Renaissance style. The interior boasts magnificent timber.*

Above: *The Gold Coast is Australia's best known tourist destination, and Surfers Paradise, a thriving centre of high-rise apartments looking out on a superb beach, lies at the heart of the area. At sunset, the surfing stops and the nightlife begins.*

Opposite top: *One of the numerous five-star resorts on the Gold Coast is the Sheraton Marina Mirage located on The Spit at Southport. It caters for both holidaymakers and the yachting fraternity and is close to many of the major attractions of the Gold Coast.*

Opposite bottom: *Although the Gold Coast enjoys the reputation of being one of Queensland's prime holiday destinations, the surfers who spend hours waiting for the perfect wave are a reminder that the area's attraction is ultimately its run of fine beaches.*

Left: *Noosa Heads is a chic holiday destination north of Brisbane. It has a quiet beach and an excellent coastal park. An exciting annual competition for outrigger canoes is held at Noosa.*
Below: *Located on the Gold Coast at Surfers Paradise, the Jupiter's Casino complex has gaming rooms, tennis courts, swimming pools and jogging tracks. Opened in 1986, the hotel has over 600 guest rooms and operates 24 hours a day.*

Above: The escarpment rises steeply behind Queensland's narrow coastal strip. This results in hundreds of waterfalls, including this attractive tropical rainforest display in the Lamington National Park near the Gold Coast.

Right: The Noosa National Park, located on the headland beyond the town's main beach, is a small coastal park of 382 hectares where birds and mammals find refuge in the native flora. The bushwalks and picnic spots are a tranquil retreat from the tourism of the surrounding area.

Right: *The freshwater lakes on the world's largest sand island, Fraser Island, are crystal clear and peaceful. Visitors to the island can swim in the lakes, lie on the pure white beaches, and camp in a number of designated campsites, including this wonderful setting at Lake Boomanjin.*

Below: *Central Station was once the home of over 100 people and the heart of the forestry industry on Fraser Island. Today, the timber walkways lead to the cool and leafy Woongoolber Creek, a small river which carries clear water through the island's rainforest. Dingoes can often be seen wandering through the bush.*

Right: After 30 years of service in Australian waters, the Maheno, *a large luxury cruise liner which had been used as a hospital ship during World War I, was being towed to Japan as scrap when it hit cyclonic conditions off the Fraser Island coast. It was subsequently washed ashore on 9 July 1935 where it lies forlornly on Fraser Island's Seventy Five Mile Beach. The repeated weathering action of the waves and the wind have reduced this once huge vessel to a rusting hulk.*

Fraser Island

Bottom right:
Recognised as
one of the most
luxurious resorts
on the Great
Barrier Reef, Hamilton Island
has a range of accommodation
from hotel suites to self-contained
apartments and huts. There is an
à la carte restaurant, a coffee shop, a
seafood restaurant, a pizza parlour,
snack bar, cocktail bar, and the
famous (or infamous) swimming pool
bar and moveable 'Booze Mobile'.
The vast complex includes a marina
for 200 boats, six swimming pools,
six tennis courts and eight bars.

Hamilton
Island

Above: The mainland centre for the
Whitsunday Islands, Airlie Beach, is
the essence of tourism with numerous
motels, resorts and camping sites.

Above right: There are few better
ways of enjoying the coral gardens of
the Great Barrier Reef than from a
glass-bottomed boat. Beneath you is
a landscape of marine wonders.

Opposite: Visitors who want to scuba
dive are transported in style on one of
many cruise ships which travel from
the Queensland coast to the outer
limits of the Great Barrier Reef.

Below left: *Away from the bustle of tourism, Queenslanders go fishing and take time out to enjoy the natural beauty of their tropical environment. Along the intricate coastline, which is extensive, it is still possible to find a small piece of paradise.*

Right: *On a summer's evening the sunsets in the Whitsundays are quite spectacular. On Hamilton Island, a magical sunset signals the beginning of the nightlife at the island's resort.*

Below: *Only 8 kilometres from Townsville, beautiful Magnetic Island has not been over-developed. There are numerous walks, both gentle and taxing, around the island, including an interesting one to Radical Bay.*

Above: *A number of Aboriginal dance companies have formed in north Queensland to entertain visitors to the area. The most famous is the Tjapukai Dance Theatre, located in both Kuranda and at the Tjapukai Aboriginal Village near the Skyrail outside Cairns.*

Opposite top: *Cairns Harbour is the main point of departure for tours to the Great Barrier Reef and the islands to the east of the city of Cairns. Cruise vessels travel to the reef each day.*

Opposite bottom left: *A delightful journey through tropical rainforest and across waterfalls, the old Cairns-to-Kuranda railway is one of the major attractions of the area.*

Opposite bottom right: *The stage curtain at the Tjapukai Dance Theatre depicts the interesting story of the Tjapukai people and the flora and fauna of the area. It features Kuranda, the centre of the Tjapukai world, undersea creatures and fruit bats which live in rainforest trees.*

Opposite: *The Great Barrier Reef, which can be seen from the moon, is the largest structure ever created by living creatures. It covers a total area of around 215 000 square kilometres and stretches along the coast for around 2000 kilometres in a series of reefs, coral cays and islands. It is home to over 350 species of coral.*

Great Barrier Reef

Top left: *The cathedral fig tree near the town of Yungaburra in the Atherton Tablelands is a top tourist attraction. By an accident of nature, it has created a vast curtain of roots which drops 15 metres from the main body of the tree to the ground.*

Top right: *The Great Barrier Reef is a coral wonderworld of over 1000 varieties of tropical fish. This coral garden is typical of the richness and diversity of this living structure.*

Above: *Daytrippers travel from Cairns to Green Island where they can relax at the resort, explore the reefs which surround the island or simply lie on the coral beach and enjoy the warm waters. The island was once uninhabited, with nothing more than a jetty. The resort has taken over Green Island's previously primitive charm; there is now a Marineland, a Barrier Reef Theatre, snorkelling trails, and a range of eating facilities.*

Above: Cooktown once had a lively, colourful past. The main street used to be 3 kilometres long and boasted over 100 pubs where hot and dusty miners, heading inland to the gold-fields, used to quench their thirst.

Right: Cooktown Harbour was first used by Captain James Cook when he was forced to repair a hole in the H. M. Bark Endeavour caused by a collision with the Great Barrier Reef. Today, the harbour is used mainly by fishermen and cruise ships.

Opposite: Cape York is the northern-most tip of Queensland. Here the warm waters of Torres Strait, the rainforest of Cape York Peninsula and the surrounding granite cliffs stare across the shallow waters separating Australia from Papua New Guinea.

Top left: *The Gulf of Carpentaria is characterised by vast distances and poor roads. Many of the landowners of huge stations use light aircraft and helicopters to locate their cattle and to move around their properties.*

Bottom left: *Cape York Peninsula is cattle country. Much of the area is ideal for livestock and a few wealthy landowners manage huge herds which roam freely across the country. Rounding up the beasts is done with trucks and four-wheel-drive vehicles.*

Right: *The area around Longreach in western Queensland is strictly cattle country. It is therefore appropriate that the Stockman's Hall of Fame, a fascinating exploration of the early days in the Australian outback, should be located just outside town.*

Below: *The Norman River runs into the Gulf of Carpentaria at Karumba, north of Normanton. Fed by the tropical 'wet', the lazy meanders of the river create fantastic shapes when viewed from the air.*

VICTORIA

Opposite: *The Yarra River flows through the bustling heart of Melbourne.*
Above: *Beside St Kilda, in Melbourne's Botanic Gardens, is a beautiful flower clock.*

Covering about 3 per cent of mainland Australia, with a surface area of only 227 620 square kilometres, Victoria is the smallest state apart from Tasmania. Despite its size, it is home to over 25 per cent of the country's population. At its heart lies the elegant and sophisticated capital city of Melbourne.

Victoria is rich in natural resources, including excellent pastureland and substantial forests. More than a third of the state is covered with forests of eucalypts, mountain and alpine ash, and significant plantations of both softwoods and hardwoods. With such an abundance of lush grazing, the state is primarily a producer of fine wool and fat lamb. Beef, wheat and dairy farming also contribute to the state's economy.

Known throughout Australia as 'The Garden State', Victoria embraces remarkably diverse landscapes. The coastline consists of 1200 kilometres of dramatic cliffs, rock arches, stacks and blowholes, stretching from Cape Otway to Port Campbell, as well as the seemingly endless expanse of sand which is Ninety Mile Beach. The Great Ocean Road, one of the most beautiful scenic drives in Australia, winds around the south-western coast for 320 kilometres. Particularly impressive are the Twelve Apostles, evidence of the corrosive powers of the mighty Southern Ocean, and the remnants of London Bridge, both lying to the west of Port Campbell.

The near-desert of the Mallee stretches to the west, while to the north the southern edges of the Snowy Mountains are dotted with popular ski resorts. Central Victoria is graced by the majestic Grampian ranges, as well as quaint towns like Ballarat and Bendigo which were created as a result of the 19th-century gold rushes. The mountainous east, which experiences significant snow falls and sub-zero temperatures in winter, gradually gives way to gently undulating slopes.

The Murray River, which accounts for most of the northern border, has done much to define the economy of the state. Once plied by steamers carrying produce to the rich Riverina sheep stations, it is now a popular holiday retreat for tourists wanting to visit the old riverbank towns.

Left: *The Rialto Towers are typical of modern Melbourne. Built in 1890, the original 19th-century Gothic facade of the building has been carefully restored, providing the perfect foil for the modern twin office towers behind.*

Above: *Melbourne's Shrine of Remembrance was designed along the same lines as the Parthenon in Athens. Being the city's main war memorial, it becomes the focal point on Anzac Day when those Victorians who died in the war are remembered.*

Opposite top: *Built in 1888, Princes Bridge crosses the Yarra River from the parks and gardens of the south bank to the heart of the city's central business district. Across the bridge lie Flinders Street Railway Station and Swanston Street.*

Opposite bottom: *Southgate, on the southern side of the Yarra River, was once an unattractive industrial area. Today this wonderful collection of restaurants, shops and cafes provides a link between the city's arts centres and the central business district.*

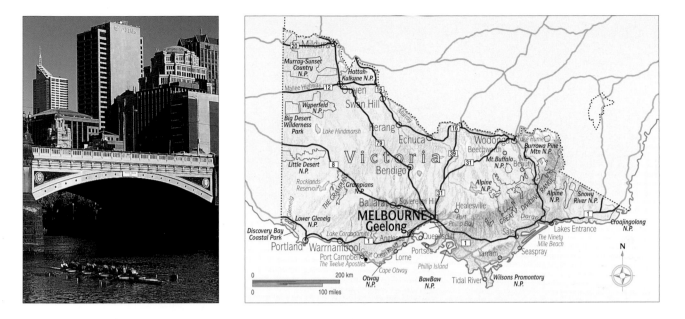

Opposite top left: *The Victorian Arts Centre is an integrated collection of buildings including the Melbourne Concert Hall, the Performing Arts Museum, the National Gallery of Victoria, and the State and Studio Playhouses building; the centre is the heart of the city's artistic life.*

Opposite top right: *The area from Southgate to the opulent Victorian Arts Centre, with its numerous venues for performances of the arts, is linked by a series of open spaces, grassed recreational parklands, restaurants, and sculptures. This sculpture typifies the artistic atmosphere of the area.*

Opposite bottom: *The heart of Melbourne is Flinders Street Railway Station where trams, trains and buses from all over the metropolitan area bring people to the city centre.*
Above: *The view from the charming bayside suburb of Williamstown, which lies south-west of Melbourne.*

Left: The Great Ocean Road is Victoria's premier tourist attraction. The picturesque route runs for 320 kilometres along the state's rugged south-western coast. The highlight of the journey is the sight of the Twelve Apostles jutting forlornly out of the southern ocean.

Twelve Apostles

Opposite top: The first Tuesday in November is Melbourne Cup day. On this famous race day the whole nation seems to come to a collective halt in order to follow the commentary on the nearest television or radio. Almost everybody gets caught up in the excitement of the event, placing bets or joining a sweep.

Opposite bottom: A remnant of 19th-century coyness and elegance, Brighton Beach still has rows of quaint, colourful bathing boxes where people can change before going swimming. Brighton Beach, with its old fashioned seaside appeal, is one of Melbourne's most refined suburbs.

Opposite: This view of Halls Gap and Lake Bellfield is a typical panorama from the spectacular range of sandstone ridges known as the Grampians. The mountains, which form part of the western edge of the Great Dividing Range, are a popular haunt for bushwalkers.

Above: Cruising along the Murray River (the northern border of Victoria) is an increasingly popular holiday activity. In the 19th century, the river was a vital transport route servicing vast areas of northern Victoria and south-western New South Wales.

Left: The shy eastern grey kangaroo is common throughout Victoria. In the wilds it can be seen grazing in the early morning and late afternoon. Eastern greys can move at speeds of up to 60 kilometres per hour.

Opposite top: *A recreation of an historic mining town, Sovereign Hill near Ballarat is a major tourist attraction. Visitors can travel by Cobb & Co. coach, or pan for gold in a nearby stream. In the evenings, there is a spectacular recreation of the battle fought at the Eureka Stockade.*

Ballarat

Opposite bottom left: *Sealers Cove at Wilsons Promontory was named after the sealers who inhabited the area. Today, there are few reminders of the unhappy past of this beautiful stretch of coastline with its famous sandy beaches and rocky headlands.*

Opposite bottom right: *The Fairy penguin is the smallest species of penguin in the world; it attains a height of only 33 centimetres. Visitors from far and wide visit the rookeries.*

Above: *Gold was first discovered in the Beechworth area in northern Victoria in 1852. Today, this mining town has a feast of historic buildings ranging from the local court house and gaol to the Commercial Hotel.*

Overleaf: *Lakes Entrance in eastern Victoria is a quiet retreat for people keen to fish in both the ocean and the nearby lakes. Below the entrance to the lakes is Ninety Mile Beach, one of the longest beaches in Australia.*

Top: *The Snowy Mountains in Victoria are covered with snow for most of the winter months, bringing hardship to the local farmers but crowds of very happy skiers to the nearby ski fields.*
Above: *Victoria's climate, particularly in the eastern half of the state, is cool. The temperate rainforests, with their heavy undergrowth of ferns and tall eucalypts, are a reflection of this.*
Right: *Each spring the snow on the Snowy Mountains melts and fills the local rivers. Although some rivers have been dammed, it is common for the upper reaches of the Murray River to flood with the melting snow.*

TASMANIA

Opposite: A view of Wineglass Bay from Mount Amos in Freycinet National Park.
Above: The apple is the symbol of Tasmania.

Tasmania, the smallest of Australia's states, defies all standard Australian images. Situated to the south of Victoria, it is separated from the mainland by the treacherous Bass Strait. Long, isolated stretches of beach on the island's west coast are subjected to the mighty waves that roll uninterrupted across the southern oceans, propelled by the icy Roaring Forties. Wet, green and distinctly European, there is a sense of 'otherness' about Tasmania.

The state, including King and Flinders islands and a number of smaller islands in Bass Strait which make up the outer limits of Tasmania, covers an area of 67 800 square kilometres. Nearly 50 per cent of the population of less than half a million lives in Hobart, the state capital. Given the wildness of the weather, Tasmania's capital city is relatively protected.

Visitors to Hobart are drawn to Constitution Dock and Salamanca Place, famous for its weekend markets and converted Georgian-style, dockside warehouses. The boats that take part in the Sydney–Hobart yacht race cross the finishing line here each year.

Around Hobart, and in the valleys of the Derwent and Huon rivers, lie numerous orchards. It is here that the bulk of the state's apples are grown, as well as apricots and lucrative crops of oil, poppies and hops. North of Hobart, the main north–south road passes through quaint, restored villages such as Ross and Richmond, en route to Launceston. Central Tasmania is made up of a plateau with a series of glacial lakes and a number of major mountains, most notably Mount Ossa, Ben Lomond, Cradle Mountain and Eldon Park, all rising above 1400 metres.

The north-west coastal strip, between Devonport and Stanley, with its famous rocky outcrop, the 'Nut', has a favourable combination of rich soils, an average rainfall of 960 millimetres and a mild climate that is ideal for beef and dairy farming, and growing crops of potatoes and peas.

There is a need to preserve Tasmania's unique fauna and flora. The Huon pine, for example, can grow for well over 2000 years. The Tasmanian devil, once found on the mainland, is now restricted to the island, while the Tasmanian tiger is perhaps still hiding in the wilderness.

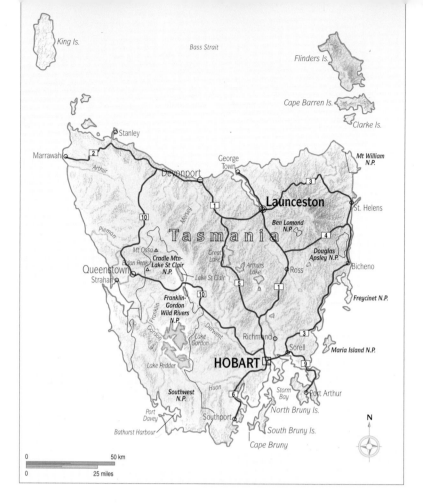

Bottom left: *Salamanca Place, once the centre of Hobart's port with its historic stone warehouses, has Tasmania's most popular weekend market. People from all over the island flock here to hunt for bargains.*

Top left: *The peaceful waters of the Derwent River, standing in stark contrast to the wild seas of Bass Strait which batter Tasmania's west coast, are ideal for sailing. The area attracts Hobart's keen sailors, as well as yachtsmen from all over the world.*

Below: *Each Australian state has its own brewery and its own beer. Few states are as proud of their beer as Tasmania. Even mainlanders will grudgingly concede that no local beer quite matches the quality of the brew produced at the Cascade Brewery.*

Above: *Located on the Derwent River, Hobart is a city of considerable beauty. Although the local casino, which was the first ever to be built in Australia, dominates the landscape, the city is better known for its large collection of historic buildings which date back to Georgian times.*

Left: *The nautical hub of Hobart is Constitution Dock. Here, sailors from all over the world arrive and, in late December, having left Sydney on Boxing Day, the tired crews of the famous Sydney—Hobart yacht race gather to celebrate its successful completion. In recent years, Constitution Dock has been the finishing line for a race that starts in Melbourne and ends in Hobart.*

Left: *The convict buildings at Port Arthur are the most successfully preserved of this kind in Australia.*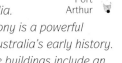
This penal colony is a powerful reminder of Australia's early history. The sandstone buildings include an unnamed church with stone spinarets and timber fittings.

Above left: *Large parts of Tasmania, of which the beautiful orange-bellied parrot is an inhabitant, are untouched wilderness areas rich in wildlife.*

Above: *A lavender crop on the Bridestowe Lavender Farm at Nabowla near Launceston.*

Opposite: *Isolated Bruny Island lies to the south of Hobart. Swept by fierce arctic winds, it has a number of reserves and national parks including this area around Cape Bruny.*

Port
Arthur

Opposite: Although commonly covered in cloud, and often covered in snow in winter, Cradle Mountain and nearby Cradle Lake in central Tasmania are quite beautiful on the rare perfect day.

Top left: The eastern pygmy possum, which lives off nectar and pollen, grows to a length of no more than 10 centimetres. It is so well adapted to Tasmania that it hibernates for most of the island's harsh winter.

Cradle Mountain

Left: Large tracts of land in Tasmania are covered with cool and temperate rainforest, a result of the winds which gust across the southern Indian Ocean bringing drenching rains to the island. Deep within these flourishing rainforests, plants like this deciduous beech and pandani are to be found.

Above: A moss-encrusted swamp eucalypt is typical of the vegetation in the rainforests on the western and south-western coasts of Tasmania. As the bush tracks tend to be dangerous and difficult to navigate, it is still a largely unexplored territory.

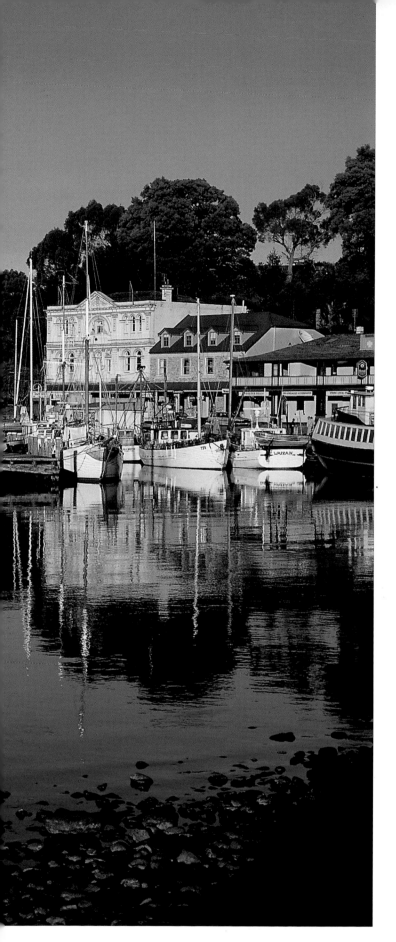

Left: *Strahan Harbour must be one of the most isolated and lonely harbours on earth. Created by the British as the ultimate penal colony, today Strahan is a small fishing and tourist township situated on the edge of the unspoiled Macquarie Harbour on Tasmania's rugged west coast.*

Above: *Across Macquarie Harbour from Strahan is the mouth of the Gordon River. One of its tributaries is the Franklin, which together with the Gordon forms the Franklin—Gordon Wild Rivers National Park. Deep within the park, the Bingham's Arch Cave can be found on the Franklin River. Although there are daily cruises across Macquarie Harbour and up the lower reaches of the Gordon River, the area is lonely and isolated. In recent times, the pristine tropical forests of this region have become popular with bushwalkers.*

Opposite: *The waves that pound unrelentingly on the harsh, flat coast near Strahan roll across the Atlantic and Indian oceans, driven by the Roaring Forties.*
Left: *The countryside to the south of Strahan is inaccessible and deserted. Seaplanes are used to travel to the isolated regions of Port Davey and Bathurst Harbour.*
Below: *At its mouth the Gordon River is edged by lush, dense rainforest where mosses and lichens cover the forest floor and grow on fallen timber.*

SOUTH AUSTRALIA

Opposite: The dramatic cliffs of the Great Australian Bight.
Above: Adelaide is known as the 'city of churches'.

South Australia is the driest of all the Australian states. With its reputation as the wine and citrus centre of the country, its prevailing image is one of fertile valleys, rolling hills and the charm of Adelaide, the 'city of churches'. The reality is that just under half of the land (476 000 square kilometres) consists of little more than harsh, unforgiving deserts of saltbush, endless sand dunes and flat, waterless lakes. In fact, only about one-third of the state—the area of the Flinders and Mount Lofty ranges, the Eyre, Yorke and Fleurieu peninsulas, the Coorong and the Murray River valley—is deemed to be economically viable. Most of this area experiences a Mediterranean climate of a moist, cold winter and a hot, dry summer; conditions weaken further inland, eventually degenerating to a point where the annual rainfall is below 125 millimetres and the summer temperatures soar above 40°C.

Situated on the banks of the slow-flowing River Torrens, Adelaide has both a country-town friendliness and a distinct big-city elegance about it. Beautiful parks and churches, and some of the best restaurants, theatres, art galleries and craft shops in the country, are among the many attractions of the capital city and surrounding area. South Australia produced the famous painter, Hans Heysen, who is remembered for his watercolours of the Australian bush, with their subtle lighting and massive, strongly drawn gum trees.

The Australian wine industry's reputation for producing quality wines was established in the valleys of South Australia. Today, the wines of the Barossa and Clare valleys, and the towns of Reynella, McLaren Vale, Penola and Coonawarra, are all internationally recognised.

South Australia's economic base includes rich deposits of uranium at Roxby Downs, open-cut coal deposits in the Leigh Creek area, natural gas in the Cooper Basin, vast iron ore deposits at Iron Knob, Iron Monarch and Iron Baron, and opal mining at Coober Pedy, Andamooka and Mintabie. Agriculturally, olives, figs, oranges, grains and sheep farming are all important.

Opposite top: *Adelaide is an elegant and charming city on the edge of the River Torrens. Unlike other Australian cities, it still has the qualities of a large country town and has not been overwhelmed by the development of its city centre.*

Opposite bottom left: *Adelaide's streetplan forms a figure eight. At the bottom of the 'main street', King William Street, is Victoria Square, the centre of the surrounding quadrants. Victoria Square, which was laid out by Colonel Light in 1837, is noted for its beautiful modern fountains.*

Opposite bottom right: *The heart of Adelaide's cultural life is the Festival Centre on the banks of Torrens Lake, which is the focus for the biennial Adelaide Arts Festival.*

Below: *South-west of Adelaide's city centre is the peaceful beach resort suburb of Glenelg with its elegant old hotels, amusement parlours, long pier and quiet family beach.*

Left: *South Australia is the country's finest grape-growing state. The vineyards near Greenoch in the Barossa Valley produce some of the state's most exceptional wines.*

Barossa Valley

Right: *The old art of barrel making, known as cooperage, still survives in the vineyards of the Clare and Barossa valleys.*

Below: *There are two species of fur seal which breed along the coast of South Australia. While some seals are permanent residents on the coast, large numbers swim north from the Antarctic and arrive in November for the breeding season.*

Right: *A popular tourist activity on the Murray River is to take a cruise on an old paddle steamer. In the late 19th century, paddle steamers plied the river, which was one of the major transport arteries of the region.*

Opposite: *When it rains (which it does rarely), the Flinders Ranges in the north of South Australia come alive with grasses and flowers. At other times they are harsh and isolated with a rugged beauty.*

Below: *Much of South Australia is desert and incapable of sustaining agriculture. Beyond the perimeters of civilisation low-lying sand dunes, hardy desert tussock grass and small bushes are typical of the landscape.*

Left: For the opal miners of Coober Pedy, digging for the precious stones is a daily grind. The intense summer temperatures and harsh conditions of the area force them to seek refuge and build their homes underground.
Right: The budgerigar, also known as the love bird or the warbling grass parakeet, is a native of the South Australian bush. During periods of drought it frequents waterholes.
Below: The train from Adelaide to Alice Springs, known as the Ghan, still runs through outback South Australia. The old railway station at Oodnadatta is now a museum recalling the early days of train travel.

Right, bottom: *Geckos are common in the deserts of South Australia. They live on insects and spiders which they catch at night, preferring to use the daylight hours to take maximum advantage of the sun.*

Following pages: *The coastline to the south of Adelaide is dry and bare during the summer months when temperatures are typically extreme. After the winter rains, grasses flourish and the land turns green. This is Sellicks Beach near Aldinga on the Fleurieu Peninsula, south of Adelaide. Fishermen drive their vehicles along the firm sand beach and launch their boats directly into the surf.*

NORTHERN TERRITORY

Opposite: *The strange rock formations known as Kata Tjuta, or the Olgas.*
Above: *Elaborately painted didgeridoos.*

There is a harsh and rugged beauty about most of the Northern Territory, a huge, sparsely populated region covering 1 346 200 square kilometres. The most enduring images left on travellers passing through the Territory are the flat, sparsely vegetated terrain, the redness of the desert soil and the overwhelming isolation. It is quite possible to drive for 200–300 kilometres without passing a single service station or seeing another human being. There are essentially only four major settlements in the Northern Territory: Darwin, Katherine, Tennant Creek and Alice Springs. Given the inhospitable nature of most of the terrain, the rest are little more than villages servicing travellers and the large properties which surround them.

Darwin and the 'Top End' are the true tropics of the Northern Territory. Each spring 'the wet' brings torrential rains to the north, filling the rivers, making many of the roads impassable and sending the humidity soaring to unbearable heights. Darwin's importance as a port, the cattle industry, and its mineral wealth have all contributed to the prosperity of this fascinating area. More recently, the natural beauty of places such as Kakadu National Park and the lesser-known Litchfield Park, with its pools and tumbling waterfalls, have contributed to the surge in tourism.

The Katherine Gorge National Park, showpiece of the Katherine area, is yet another natural wonder of spectacular proportions. Excellent swimming holes, hot springs at Mataranka and limestone formations that produced the Cutta Cutta Caves are just a few of the attractions.

Alice Springs epitomises the unique beauty of the Territory. The MacDonnell Ranges sprawl to the east and west of 'The Alice', the name given to Alice Springs by the local inhabitants. Jagged, blood-red cliffs stand out in vivid contrast against deep blue skies and the white ghost gums that grow in abundance in the region. There is endless scope for bushwalking through Ormiston Gorge and Pound, around the rim of Kings Canyon, or to the mine sites at Arltunga. To the south, the great monoliths of Uluru, or Ayers Rock, and Kata Tjuta (the Olgas) loom out of the flat wastelands of the desert, attracting visitors from far and wide.

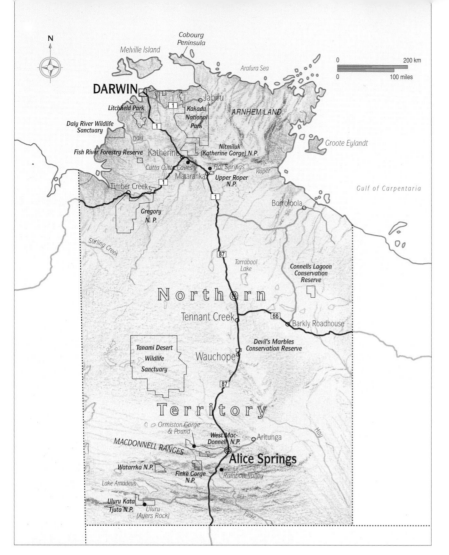

Above: The modern Parliament House building in Darwin has become a symbol of the independence and prosperity of the Northern Territory. Situated only a short distance from Government House, Parliament House has an impressive pillared facade.

Far left: Located in the park behind Mindil Beach in Darwin, the Mindil Market is a vibrant meeting place where the true multicultural nature of this tropical city can be experienced.

Left: Darwin's Government House is a timber building surrounded by palm trees and lush tropical gardens. There are also excellent views from the house across Port Darwin.

Right: Darwin's most popular family beach is Mindil Beach. Located between Bullocky Point and Myilly Point, it looks across Fannie Bay. Behind the beach is the city's casino.

Above: *Kakadu National Park's primary appeal is that it is a tropical wetlands area rich in animal life. Visitors to Kakadu are taken on cruises through the wetlands where they can observe the birdlife and see the numerous estuarine crocodiles which inhabit the park's rivers.*

Kakadu National Park

Right: *During the wet season the tropical rains fill the rivers in Kakadu National Park and Arnhem Land, and the waterfalls, which have usually been reduced to a mere trickle during the dry winter months, are galvanised into rushing torrents.*

Top right: *The lakes, swamps and riverlands of Kakadu are transformed into a wonderland of flowers after the summer rains. Exotic lilies edge the lakes and a profusion of tropical orchids grow in the swamplands.*
Right: *The vicious estuarine crocodile (Crocodylus porosus) is common to most of the Northern Territory's major rivers and freshwater swamps. A powerful and extremely dangerous carnivorous creature, it has been known to kill humans. It feeds mostly on fish, reptiles, birds, mammals and crustaceans and breeds during the wet season between January and March. Up to 50 eggs are laid and they hatch 12 weeks later.*

Bottom and right:
The Devil's Marbles Conservation Reserve lies on either side of the Stuart Highway some 10 kilometres north of Wauchope in the Northern Territory. The strange egg-shaped rocks were considered by the local Aborigines to have been actual eggs laid by the Rainbow Serpent during the Dreamtime.

Below: *Lizards abound in the desert areas of central Australia. They live in rock crevices and survive on a diet of insects and sometimes berries. It is common to see them beside the road or lying in the hot desert sun.*

Above: The Alice Springs Telegraph Station lies just north of Alice Springs. The repeater station which was built in the town in 1871–72 was the first European building to be constructed in central Australia.

Opposite top: Each year the people of Alice Springs celebrate the dryness of central Australia with a satiric boat race down the Todd River. Named the Henley-on-Todd, the race is run on the dry bed of the Todd River and aptly illustrates the 'Top End's' eccentricity.

Opposite bottom: Camels, originally brought to Australia by Afghan camel drivers for exploration purposes, are still used today as an unusual form of transportation for tourists.

Right: The Royal Australian Flying Doctor service was created by the Reverend John Flynn to bring medical assistance to people in the outback.

Opposite: *The MacDonnell Ranges, stretching to the east and west of Alice Springs, are ancient remnants of a mountain range that was once much higher than the Himalayas. Millions of years of weathering have reduced the range to a rocky outcrop.*
Left: *Many of central Australia's Aborigines still live a traditional life. In recent times land claims have allowed them their independence and dignity.*

Below: *Road trains are notoriously dangerous and it is advisable to head for the bush if you see one coming along a dirt or single-track road.*
Bottom: *The scenery of the Northern Territory is impossible to forget. The redness of the desert, the blueness of the sky and the jagged harshness of the mountain ranges is like nothing else on earth. This is an area in the Territory known as Rainbow Valley.*

Far left: *The Glen Helen Gorge, cut away by the Finke River, is important to the Aboriginal mythology of the area as it was from here that some of the creatures of the Dreamtime emerged.*

Left: *The Olgas are now known as Kata Tjuta, which means 'head' and 'many' in the language of the traditional owners. These huge rocky outcrops are noted for their engravings and geometric rock piles which local Aborigines believe were created by the Spirit Ancestor during the Dreamtime.*

Below: *The main attraction at the top of Kings Canyon is the 'Lost City', a series of ancient weathered buttresses of rock which look like the ruins of an ancient city, although some visitors are more inclined to describe it as a moonscape.*

Above: The decision to walk to the top of Uluru is one which should be based on fitness and your level of respect for the Aboriginal notion that this is a sacred site. As the traditional owners of the rock, they believe that people should not walk on it. Each year, tens of thousands of tourists choose to make the climb.

Right: In the language of the local Aborigines, the name 'Uluru' is applied to both the rock and the waterhole on top of it. The rock rises 348 metres above the surrounding countryside, has an area of 3.33 square kilometres and a total circumference of 9.4 kilometres. It is an awesome sight, especially when the sun is rising or setting.

WESTERN AUSTRALIA

Opposite: *Lake Argyle is Australia's largest man-made reservoir.*
Above: *The short-beaked echidna, or spiny anteater.*

Covering an unbelievable 2 525 500 square kilometres with nearly 7000 kilometres of rugged coastline, Western Australia is the largest state in Australia. It is an extensive, low-lying plateau, rarely rising above 600 metres—the only exceptions being the narrow coastal plain which runs down the west coast from Broome to Albany, the Stirling Range in the south, and the iron-ore-rich Hamersley Range in the north-west.

The climate varies dramatically in Western Australia. In the north the monsoonal wet season sweeps across Wyndham, the Kimberley and the Broome area between December and March, making roads impassable and filling the area's crocodile-infested rivers. The town of Marble Bar symbolises the extreme climatic variation prevalent across this vast region. Known as the hottest place in Australia, the longest heat wave ever recorded in the town was from 31 October 1923 to 17 April 1924, when the temperature remained a constant 100°F (38°C).

Beyond the coastal plain, most of Western Australia is an endless, largely uninhabited desert, with the Great Sandy Desert covering 258 000 square kilometres alone. In the south the desert landscape is transformed by a mild Mediterranean climate of cool, wet winters and warm, dry summers, providing an ideal environment for the production of verdant timberlands.

It is hardly surprising that over 90 per cent of the population lives in the fertile south-west region which encompasses the charming cities of Perth and Fremantle. Characterised by a coastline of breathtaking beauty, where huge sand dunes carpeted with wildflowers butt up against dramatic granite headlands, this is one of the most beautiful areas in Australia. Cable Beach, an isolated resort near Broome, stands alone on a deserted shore. North of Perth, the cliffs of Kalbarri tower above the sea and the sentinel-like Pinnacles, a natural rock formation, pierce the sky near the town of Cervantes in the Nambung National Park. Inland, huge karri and jarrah hardwood forests surround the small timber towns nestling in valleys, and wisps of blue smoke from the sawmills punctuate the grey-green of the surrounding vegetation.

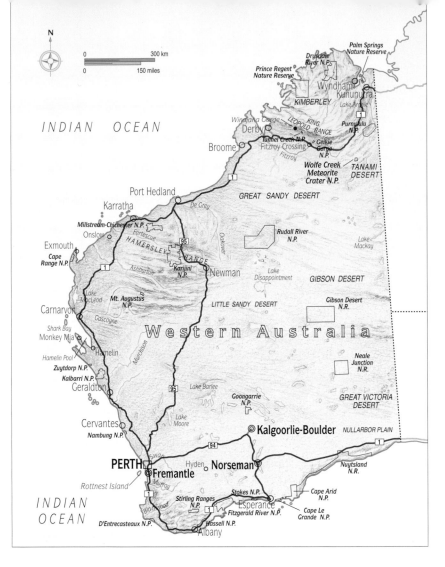

Opposite bottom: *The University of Western Australia has a beautiful location on the Swan River at Nedlands. Winthrop Hall is one of its most distinctive buildings with a clock tower that dominates the campus.*

Left: *London Court in Perth is a shopping alley with a mock Tudor frontage. Built in 1938 by Claude de Bernales, it is a popular meeting place for people shopping in the Hay Street Pedestrian Mall.*

Below: *Kings Park, otherwise known as Mount Eliza, offers a superb view of Perth and the graceful Swan River. In the distance the modern high-rise buildings are a reminder of the earlier dynamism of the city.*

Right: *Kings Park has been a source of pleasure to Perth residents since it was set aside as parkland in 1831 by the colony's first Surveyor General, John Septimus Roe. The gardens have stands of jarrah, karri and heath.*

Above: Rottnest Island is Perth's favourite holiday destination. Only 12 minutes by air and 2 hours by water, the island is an accessible location for anybody wishing to escape from the city. It offers quiet beaches and historic buildings.

Right: Almost a suburb of Perth, Fremantle lies at the mouth of the Swan River. Once little more than a port it is now a refined centre.

Opposite: Fremantle has a wealth of important historic buildings. Elegant colonial buildings, such as this one, were built by convicts in the period from 1850 until 1868 as part of a widescale building program.

Above: *The King Leopold Ranges in the Kimberley region in the north of the state are typical of the vastness, loneliness and harshness of much of Western Australia.*

Right: *The isolated town of Broome was once a pearl fishing port. In recent times Lord McAlpine, one-time confidante of Margaret Thatcher and senior British Conservative Party politician, has bought up many of the town's historic buildings and has built a five-star resort at Cable Beach.*

Right: One of
Western Australia's
most distinctive
landforms is Wave

Rock at Hyden in
the wheatbelt. The rock, which
is over 100 metres long, is like a
huge breaking wave. This unusual
shape was caused by weathering of
the rock below the ground before it
was exposed. Its remarkable shape is
highlighted by vertical streaks of
algae growing on the surface.
Below: Geikie Gorge is 15 kilometres
to the north of the Fitzroy Crossing in
the Kimberley. Together with Tunnel
Creek and Windjana Gorge, it forms
part of an ancient 'barrier reef' which
developed during the Devonian Period
about 350 million years ago.

Previous pages: East of Perth, most of the landscape consists of wheatbelt country. Visitors can travel hundreds of kilometres through fields of wheat which stretch to the distant horizon. The only break in the monotony are the scores of tiny wheatbelt towns which usually boast a single pub, the ubiquitous general store and a farm machinery sales yard.

Above: At Monkey Mia, on the coast of Shark Bay, dolphins come ashore regularly to be fed and to play with the thousands of visitors who are attracted to the region each year. In the early 1960s, a woman named Mrs Watts started feeding the school of wild dolphins which used to follow her husband's fishing boat to a small campsite on the shoreline.

Opposite top: At Hamelin Pool on Shark Bay, domed stromatolites have formed on the water's edge. These strange formations are created by single-celled organisms called cyan-bacteria which grow at a rate of less than 1 millimetre per year.
Opposite bottom: Beautiful yellow paper daisies adorn parts of Western Australia in spring.

Opposite: The Kalgoorlie Museum of the Goldfields, which offers excellent views from its lookout at the top of the Ivanhoe headframe, gives an excellent introduction to the history of the area by highlighting the wealth of the early township, its local union movement and the desert flora.

Above: The Pinnacles near Cervantes rate as one of Western Australia's most unusual natural landforms. These strange, much-photographed limestone pillars look like no other landscape in Australia. They stand like silent sentinels on a plain of wind-blown sand.

The
Pinnacles

Above: *Wildflowers grow in abundant profusion beside the roads and in the national parks and nature reserves in the southern parts of Western Australia. The rich floral displays reach their peak between August and September. To see the wildflowers, it is best to follow the nature trails which wind through many of the national parks. It is estimated that there are over 12 000 species, of which over 8 000 have been named.*

INDEX

Page references in *italic* refer to photographs.